CHAPTER 1

Preparing for the Long Haul

• •

*Z*ero hour has arrived. You and your family are about to be introduced to the church. You're sitting on the platform (a bit edgy), waiting to preach your first sermon to your new church. Your family is trying to look its best in spite of the stress involved in leaving dear Christian friends and perhaps family, packing and unpacking, beginning a new ministry, learning a new congregation, buying a new home, finding a new doctor, getting the children started in school, and a thousand other things. You know the story. You may have been through it before, or this may be your first time.

You look into the people's faces and wonder, *What are they thinking; what do they expect from me and my family?* You glance around the interior of the sanctuary, listen to the music, sing some, and wonder how your family is taking all this. You make a last-minute check of your notes and mentally get ready to preach.

The chairperson of the search committee has walked to the pulpit and is saying, "This is our new pastor," or, "This is our new minister of music," or minister of education, or youth, or whatever your title and ministry may be. (I remember the pride and anxiety I felt each time I heard that introduction.) You take a deep breath and pray the service will go well, the people will be blessed, and God will be honored.

In spite of the tension, you feel a deep sense of pride and excitement in knowing this is your church and you are this congregation's pastor. They have called you; they wanted you; they felt you were God's choice for them. Already you are beginning to feel this is your church family. You are going to love them, and they are going to love you—most of them, that is. The excitement in the chairperson's voice adds to your sense of pride and satisfaction in knowing that you, your family, and this congregation are about to begin a wonderful journey of service in God's kingdom.

Whether this is your first church or a new church to which God has called you, the critical question is, "Now that I'm here, what's the best way for me to get started in this new ministry?" Let me put you at ease: Whether this is your first ministry position or a change of ministry, the principles of a good beginning are the same.

Experienced pastors should have a higher level of wisdom and a lower level of anxiety as they begin new ministries. On the other hand, they may be carrying burdensome baggage from bad past experiences. A new beginning is a good time to sort through the experiences of the past, to save what is good and discard what is not. Every pastor should follow Paul's wise action: Forget "those things which are behind [that need forgetting], and [reach] forth unto those things which are before." Press "toward the mark for the prize of the high calling of God in Christ Jesus" (Phil. 3:13–14) in your new ministry.

This congregation is new. It is not the same as your previous church. It may be better; it may not be as good. One thing is certain—it will be different. Learn from your past experiences. Draw on them for help as you face the future. Good experiences are to be cherished. They will affirm you in difficult times and guide you as you move forward. Other experiences need to be dealt with once and for all, laid down, and left behind. You, your family, and your new church deserve the freshness of a new beginning. This is one of the great blessings of a new place of service. Sometimes debriefing with a trusted friend can help you filter through your past, save what you should, and forget what you must.

If this is your first church, take heart. God will use you in amazing ways to grow His kingdom. As I look back on the early years of my ministry, I am amazed at what God accomplished through me. I was so eager and energetic that I didn't know "it couldn't be done." God guided, encouraged, and forgave me as I moved forward in His kingdom's work; and He will do the same for you.

You have much to learn. Don't try to hide your inexperience from your people. (They'll find out anyway.) Sincerely ask for their help. They will respond eagerly. Your openness and honesty will build a sense of trust in the congregation and will produce a team spirit from which you will learn leadership principles that will stay with you for the rest of your ministry.

God calls persons into ministry, and He actively involves Himself in the process of calling pastors to particular places of service. You are at your particular place at this particular time because God has special plans to use you in a particular way. Indeed, in the will of God, "thou art come to [this church] for such a time as this" (Esth. 4:14). Keep the sense of your calling fresh. Review it often. Occasionally remind the congregation of how God worked to bring the two of you together.

> **You are at your particular place at this particular time because God has special plans to use you in a particular way.**

As God works in your life and in your church, update the story of your call. Revisit those unique events—the timing, the circumstances, and the feelings you, your family, the search committee, and the church experienced—through which God led you to become that church's pastor. These events could not have been coincidences. God worked in His own unique way to bring your present ministry into being. Sometimes He worked with your knowledge and active participation; sometimes He surprised you. How exciting and wonderful it is to know that God brought you to where you are. This is your divinely ordained place of kingdom leadership.

You may be thinking, *Yes, I agree with all you say and I glory in it, but how do I begin?*

A good place to begin is to remember that you are a vital part of God's great, growing kingdom. You are not alone. You are part of a mighty army of God's servants, and your church is an outpost of His kingdom.

Dr. Gene Mims, Vice President of the Church Growth Group of the Baptist Sunday School Board, reminds us in *Kingdom Principles for Church Growth* that the driving force for church growth is the Great Commission. Five basic functions of the church—evangelism, discipleship, ministry, fellowship, and worship—are involved in accomplishing the Great Commission. As a kingdom leader, you are responsible for providing balanced leadership in these five areas.

However, don't hesitate to ask for the congregation's help or to share the work of the ministry with them. Make this practice your ministry lifestyle. If you do, you and your people will be blessed; and the church will grow.

The degree to which you assume direct leadership responsibility or share that responsibility with others will depend on your spiritual gifts, the size and gifts of your staff, and the size and gifts of your congregation. However, the more you share leadership responsibility with your congregation, the more effective your ministry will be. If you have a tendency to do it all and to control everything, get over it. Don't feel guilty because you share the work of ministry with others, but don't get the idea that letting others do the work gets you off the hook. You are their leader, and you should not ask your people to do anything you will not and do not do.

God has provided or will provide the congregation with every gift necessary for that church to do His will. You will discover that your people have exactly the gifts needed for the church to carry out the Great Commission. Therefore, make a conscious effort to discover and to help individuals discover and use their spiritual gifts. Sometimes you can make this discovery through experience and observation, but you may want to use a ministry gifts inventory such as the one contained in *Kingdom Principles Growth Strategies*.

The entire "strategies" module, Item number 5600–04, and the *Ministry Gifts Inventory,* Item number 5600–38, are available through the Customer Service Center, Baptist Sunday School Board, 1–800–458–2772.

Your leadership model is Jesus Christ. And, while your church is the immediate arena of your service, God's kingdom is the greater realm of your service. Dr. Michael D. Miller, Director of the Church Leadership Services Division of the Baptist Sunday School Board, in his book *Kingdom Leadership* states that the kingdom of God is "the reign of God through Jesus Christ in the lives of persons, as evidenced by God's activity in, through, and around them."[1]

Kingdom leaders' motivation is dramatically different from that of secular leaders. Although the church must follow good business practices, it is not a business corporation and must not operate like one. The head of the church is Jesus Christ, and His will is supreme. He is the Great Shepherd of the sheep; we are undershepherds. We are to walk like He walked and to lead like He led. Our motive is neither money, production, nor numbers. Money is useful and even essential in ministry; numbers are an indication of our effectiveness as leaders; but our motive must be Christ-centered servant-leadership that rises out of our call to salvation, our call to ministry, and our call to a particular place of service. If you are uncertain about any of these calls in your life or the nature of your ministry, take the issue to the Lord in prayer, study your Bible, and perhaps take counsel with a wise and trusted friend until the doubt is resolved.

Your motive for ministry must rise out of your call to salvation, your call to ministry, and your call to your particular place of service.

Can a local church be a part of God's kingdom growth without seeing significant numerical growth in the congregation? Absolutely! All churches may not experience numerical growth, but all churches can experience spiritual growth and can be healthy participants in kingdom growth. Carrying out the Great Commission results in numerical growth in most places, but churches exist in communities where the population is declining. If persons are being won to Christ and lives are being changed through a church's ministry, kingdom growth is occurring there even though those persons may not be added to that church's membership. Your church may win people to Christ and then see them move away and join another church. If that happens, take heart! You and your church are partners with God in the growth of His kingdom. Remember, His kingdom is immensely greater than any church or group of churches. Therefore, you must see your ministry as a part of that kingdom. Otherwise, you lose sight of what true biblical ministry is all about—the growth of God's mighty kingdom, not just the growth of a local church.

As you begin your new ministry, believe in kingdom growth, focus on Jesus as your model, get with your Bible, and get going!

The Bible is God's inerrant, infallible Word. It is the most practical book ever written. It is a splendid book of organization, direction, and purpose. It addresses every spiritual and moral need. The Bible answers every question we can think to ask and even those we aren't wise enough to ask. It gives wise counsel in areas some might consider secular. For example, the Book of Nehemiah is the best business administration book ever written. All corporate leaders ought to be students of that book.

The New Testament reveals that Jesus was a well-organized person. No one ever accomplished as much in as little time as Jesus did. He not only gave the Great Commission, He practiced it. Jesus called to Himself 12 disciples and designated them "apostles." He divided the Twelve into teams of twos and sent them out "to preach the kingdom of God" (Luke 9:1–2). Then He increased the number to 70. He also divided the 70 into teams of twos and sent them "into every city and place, whither He Himself would come" (Luke 10:1). Many other examples could be cited of Jesus practicing the principle of allowing pupils to learn by doing. If Jesus practiced that principle, shouldn't we?

Another book of the Bible that often is overlooked in its emphasis on organization, patterns, focus, and direction is Psalms. As a nonmusician, I confess to being surprised by this. I shouldn't have been. After all, no communication is more precise in its design than music. I discovered the wise administrative counsel Psalm 126 gives years ago while preaching through the psalm. The Lord suddenly spoke to me, and I said (probably out loud), "That's it! God has given an administrative plan that is simple enough for me to understand and follow." The more I study Psalm 126, the more I'm convinced that it provides a basic pattern for giving leadership in kingdom ministry. I especially commend this great psalm as a pattern of kingdom leadership.

Let's look at what this wonderful psalm has to offer. As we do, please relate it's truths to the ministry that God has given you. He has called you to be a kingdom leader, and He wants to use you to help grow His kingdom.

Visualize the Joy of Your Ministry

The psalmist was deliriously happy as he visualized in his mind's eye God's miraculous deliverance of Israel from imminent destruction. The singer exclaimed, "When the Lord turned again the captivity of Zion, we were like them that dream. Then was our mouth filled with laughter, and our tongue with singing: then said they among the heathen, the LORD hath done great things for them. The LORD hath done great things for us; whereof we are glad" (Ps. 126:1–3).

The inspired writer may have been remembering God's mighty deliverance of Israel from Egyptian bondage. He may have been thinking about the night when God delivered Jerusalem from the Assyrians during the reign of King Hezekiah. Or, he may have been celebrating God's gracious care of the Israelites while in Babylonian captivity and their return to the promised land. Whatever the occasion, the psalmist was joyously reliving the event. The experience was so real to him that in his heart he went back to that magnificent day and became a part of what God did.

As the psalmist celebrated this great event of the past, his overwhelming hope was that God would do it again. Many of us live with that same hope: "Lord, do it again!"

Part of your mission as a God-called pastor is to visualize what He wants you to do in your particular place at this particular time. Therefore, visualize with joy the victories God already has given you and those He is going to give you in your ministry. Take time to rehearse the times when you have seen God do a great work in the life of a church. Add to that the testimonies that you have heard and read of God's great work in other places. Then focus on the special place to which God has called you. Remember, He has placed you, uniquely you, at that place at this time. And, He wants you to catch a vision for the ministry He longs for you to have to and through your church. The church to which God has called you is His church, but in a sense it is your church. God has given you this assignment. You should be asking God, "Lord, how can I see what You have in mind for me and my church now and in the future? How can I become Your visionary leader?"

Set a Pace You Can Keep

Your ministry at your new church should not be a 100-yard dash. It should be a marathon. So, run "with patience," with the power to stay in the race to the finish.

Your excitement level is high. You are anxious to get to work, to make a good impression, to see things happen. Relax. Be yourself. Spend time with your family. They also have been affected by the move. Your new responsibilities are very serious, but don't take yourself too seriously. Laugh a little. Tell or listen to a funny story. Take a little time to do something familiar. Play your guitar; shoot a basketball; hang a few pictures; do something to relax. Let this be the pattern of your first few weeks at your new church. Obviously, some ministry things must be done, but all the shut-ins don't have to be visited the first month you're there. They were getting by before you arrived. All those things that need to be done, do not have to be done immediately. Be sure that what you do is in response to God's call and for His glory, not for the enhancement of your own pastoral self-image.

Begin to do those things that must be done in the short term. Visit the critically ill. If a great "saint" of the church is a shut-in, a visit or two might be strategic. Make friends with at least one lost or unchurched person. Block out some time to pray and prepare your sermons. Don't let the excitement and high energy generated by the newness of your church cause you to try to do too much too soon or to feel guilty because you can't get it all done at once.

Don't accept all the social invitations you receive as the new pastor. Politely push some of these into the future. Don't fill your schedule with pastoral sessions with those who have chronic problems. Most of all, don't you believe or let them believe that because you're their new pastor, you can cure all their problems with your expertise. Be careful about allowing yourself to be elected to an office in any of the scores of good organizations or causes outside the church. These organizations and causes always are looking for new leaders, and it's always open season on new pastors. Keep your focus narrow. Remember why you are where you are. Do everything you can to keep things on an even keel.

As you settle into the pace of your ministry, figuratively look at yourself in a mirror (occasionally look in a real one) and say to yourself, "God brought me here, and He is going to use me for His glory." Make that statement the focus of your life, and let it guide you unerringly through your ministry.

Prepare to Stay a Lifetime

Realistically, you probably are not going to spend the rest of your life where you are. The core issue, however, is not length of tenure; it's attitude. For God to use you best, you need to think long-term. As a God-called pastor, you should love and minister to your present church as if it were the only one God will ever give you to love and lead. This attitude will compel you to accept them for who and what they are. And, you will discover that they will accept you for who and what you are as well. This attitude does not mean you are to ignore their sins. When you preach, preach the whole counsel of God. Preach against sin, but do so eye to eye, face to face. Put yourself on the same level with them. Don't look down on them or preach down to them as one who feels enlightened, superior, and above them. Remember, you sit where they sit. You are a sinner, too.

Love and minister to your present church as if it were the only one God will ever give you.

Often our pronouns reveal our true feelings. If, when you preach about sins, shortcomings, service, or even the future of the congregation, your favorite pronoun is "you" instead of "we," you convey the message of a short-term, passing-through ministry. Pronouns like "we" and "us" often communicate far more than the mere word being spoken. These inclusive pronouns say, "We're in this together."

Begin your new ministry as you intend to continue. I suggest you not begin by spending 40 hours in visitation the first week you're at your new church unless you expect to visit 40 hours a week for the rest of your ministry. This is not a call to laziness; it's a call to pace yourself. Laziness has no place in the ministry.

Be careful about doing anything over and above normal pastoral ministry for one member unless you are prepared to do the same for all members for the rest of your time in your church. Once Caesar gave the Romans free corn and circuses, he never could take them away.

Be careful, especially in the early period of your ministry, not to create unrealistic expectations. For example, a pastor friend of mine who was serving in a rural church discovered that he was spending virtually all of his time transporting members to the doctor and grocery store. How did he get into this predicament? He began his ministry at that church by transporting those who asked, and the problem just grew and grew. Were these needs legitimate? Certainly. Did the pastor need to be spending his time this way? No. Other members could have ministered to these needs, and the pastor could have devoted his time to more primary ministries (Acts 6:1–7). Certainly the pastor needed to model biblical ministry, but God did not call him to that church to be at the beck and call of members' wants and, perhaps, whims.

If potentially controversial issues exist that were not clarified in the process of your call, deal with these early in your ministry, but deal with them gently and lovingly. If you do not deal with these issues early in your ministry, you probably will have to live with them for the rest of your ministry in this particular church. For example, your marriage policy likely needs to be stated early. Do you require a certain number of discussion sessions with the couple before you perform their ceremony? Do you perform ceremonies for those who are not members of your church? Do you conduct weddings for those who are divorced?

I am not suggesting what your practices should be. I simply am saying that you need to study the issues theologically and practically, be comfortable with you position, be prepared to live with it, and share it early on with the congregation. The best time to do this is during the process of your call to the church.

Early in my ministry, I followed the practice of not performing wedding ceremonies for divorced persons. However, after several years of turning down persons in that situation, I became convinced that, for me, this practice was not best. By refusing to perform the marriage ceremony of members of my church who were divorced, I was forcing them to be married by someone else, often without any pastoral guidance and certainly without support from their pastor and often their church. Then my dilemma became: If I change my policy now, what about all of those couples I have refused to marry? How will they feel? My solution was to wait until I changed churches to change my policy.

My intent is not to dwell on the issue of divorce and remarriage. My intent is to encourage you to think through and establish with your church how you are going to practice ministry. Most issues are easier to deal with if they are settled and properly communicated to the church at the beginning of your ministry there. Later on, issues will become attached to personalities and will be more emotionally charged.

In your heart and mind, from the beginning, prepare to stay a long time at the church to which God has called you. He may move you sooner than you think or want. If God chooses to move you at various points in your ministry, perhaps to spheres of greater service, wonderful. Accept with joy His leadership. But while you are where you are, love and serve the Lord and the people with all your heart and leave your future to Him.

Build Strong Personal Relationships

A new place of ministry means leaving behind cherished relationships of the past and building new ones. This new beginning can enhance the core relationships of who you are.

Build your relationship with God.—Very likely your new ministry will bring with it a sense of inadequacy on your part. This is normal and can be good. Your feelings of anxiety and inadequacy as you face new responsibilities can be a wonderful opportunity to draw nearer to God. God makes us aware of His presence in special ways as we face God-sized tasks. So, don't get too busy for a daily quiet time to seek His face and to ask for His help.

Build your relationship with your family.—Share your dreams, fears, and joys with those who moved with you and who will go with you when you move away. Do not place unrealistic expectations on your family. My brother, your wife is your wife. She is not the assistant pastor of the church. The church did not get two for the price of one. Make sure the two of you have agreed on her role and your relationships with each other in your ministry. The pastor's wife is to be her own person. She, like her pastor husband and all other church members, is to serve Christ within her relationship to Him. She is to be a committed church member who serves according to her gifts and opportunities. Protect the agreements that you have made with each other.

Some years ago I was talking with a search committee that had asked, I thought, every conceivable question when one of the members asked, "And what about your wife?" I responded, "She suits me just fine" (And she does!). Certainly, your ministries as a godly couple will complement each other, and you will serve together; but before God, the two of you need to decide what the details of that outlook mean. Don't let others' expectations make those decisions for you.

Be realistic in your expectations of your children. "Bring them up in the nurture and admonition of the Lord" (Eph. 6:4) because you are a Christian parent, not primarily because you are a pastor. Don't say to your children, "You can't do that because you're the pastor's child." Wouldn't it be better to say, "You shouldn't do that because it does not meet our standards as a Christian family"? Later on guidance can be given to your children in light of their own relationship with Christ and Christian maturity. Along the way, let your children see the joys of being in a pastor's home. Look for opportunities to focus your children's attention on the blessings of being in the ministry. I'm not suggesting a formal teaching approach; I'm suggesting letting the good side of God's calling and your ministry show through. God may use this to call your children into the ministry.

> **The more you know about your church's history, the better prepared you are to be its leader.**

Make time for your family. This involves quantity as well as quality of time. Write family events into your ministry calendar. This will not be easy, and you will have to miss some important events involving your family; but do your best to be present at special times. You can announce at the beginning of a committee meeting, "I apologize, but I must leave early; my daughter has a piano concert." You'll likely be respected by the committee for your decision, and your presence will mean so much to your daughter.

I literally arrived 10 minutes late for a revival service where I was the evangelist so that I could watch my son pitch one more inning of baseball. I have left meetings early to be present for cheerleading competition to support my daughter's performance. You'll be glad you made time for your children! For "When the sun sets on your ministry, your greatest heritage will be your family."[2]

Build your relationship with your church.—The more you know about your church, the better prepared you are to lead. Unless you were involved in your church's actual beginning, it has a history—most of which you likely do not know. Whether the church is 10 years old or 100 years old, how it began still affects its relationships and personality. Past major decisions made by the congregation, pastors, staff persons, or dominant individuals and families as well as theological and functional patterns that have developed all affect how you can best do ministry.

Some of the things you learn from the church's history will be positive, and some will be negative. How does knowing these things help?

In most cases, what has happened in a church's past will not prevent doing a particular ministry, but it may affect the way the ministry can best be done. For example, if the church has experienced building an unsuitable or problem building, been divided over a building program, or had trouble paying for a building project, you need to know that, especially if you're anticipating beginning a building program. If the church has experienced a serious breach in its fellowship, even if it was years ago, it's helpful to know what happened. If the church has experienced immorality or dishonesty on the part of a pastor or staff person, that experience will affect the church's trust level toward leadership for years to come. You need to know who was pastor when the church was perceived to have had its greatest days. What were his personality and ministry style like? What were his convictions? What kind of leadership did your immediate predecessor provide? How did the church respond to him? How do your ministry style and his complement each other or contrast with each other? The more you know about your church, the better you can love and lead the people.

Sometimes knowing the history of the church can be of great value. When I was attempting to call Central Baptist Church, Winchester, Kentucky, back to an emphasis on evangelism, being able to refer back to a day when a revival meeting lasted for weeks and more than 100 persons received Christ as Savior helped me immensely. A high week in my ministry at Central Baptist Church came out of a revival meeting, which we scheduled to correspond with the founding of the church 85 years before. We met in the church's old auditorium and celebrated the past, but we primarily focused on re-dreaming the dream. God used that event to draw the congregation together to re-emphasize its evangelistic purpose.

Southside Baptist Church, Princeton, Kentucky, was only 10 years old when I become its pastor. Many of the charter members were still there. Knowing the church's history and being able to draw on its early vision was of tremendous value in moving the church into an era of growth. Every church has a history that is unique. Just as surely as you have a background that helps make you who you are, so does the church.

Churches have personalities. A church's personality is formed by its geographic location as well as by its past. Its personality may be affected most by the culture of the area or by the location of its building. A church can develop an inferior attitude of being on "the other side of the tracks," or it can develop an inflated ego at being the downtown main street church. On the other hand, many churches have risen above the limitations of their location by believing that the entire surrounding area is theirs to possess for the glory of God. Personalities of churches also come from socioeconomic conditions, educational levels, the personalities of dominant members, and the leadership style of their pastors and staffs, as well as lay leaders.

The more you know about your church's personality, the better you can minister.

Churches go through experiences similar to individuals. Churches experience rejection, affirmation, and various combinations of the two. Congregations may have learned to trust or mistrust based on their experiences. Many, many factors go into the makeup of a church's personality. The more you know about your church's personality, the better you can minister.

How do you gather information on your church? By reading, observing, and listening. Listen carefully; talk even more carefully. Be careful about criticizing persons or events of the past. You were not there and might not have done any better if you had been. Don't be critical of your predecessors, and be cautious about listening to those who are critical. They may interpret your silent listening as agreeing with their criticism. On the other hand, you usually do not need to defend your predecessor unless criticism becomes extreme. Usually it's best simply to say something that is truthful but non-judgmental, such as, "I really don't know much about that. It occurred before my time." Sometimes what is said may be true; at other times it may not be. Virtually always the information has been filtered through the views of the person speaking. In fact, the information may have been filtered through the views of any number of persons who have repeated the story. Even so, such information can help you get a feel for the past and the personality of the church.

A young pastor, whose ego was running rampant, speaking of his predecessor, said in the presence of a faithful member, "They tell me Brother Bill wasn't much of a preacher." The member responded, "He may not have been, but his sermons never failed to help me." The young pastor later discovered that the member was one of the former pastor's strongest supporters. This casual, thoughtless statement became a barrier between the member and the young pastor for the rest of his tenure in that church.

You do not need to speak often of your predecessors, but when you do be sure it's complementary. The old saying, "If you can't say something good, don't say anything at all" certainly applies here. By the way, if you do not already know, you'll discover that the people who loved and supported the previous pastor likely will love and support you. And those who criticize the former pastor likely will become your critics.

Build your relationship with the community.—As you open your bank account, establish utility connections, go to the grocery store, and do other routine things to get settled, introduce yourself. Learn about people. Ask nonthreatening questions and listen to the responses. Questions such as, "Have you lived here all your life?" or "How do you like living here?" can yield a wealth of information about residents' attitudes and opinions about your new home. Of course, this also is a good time to ask, "Where do you attend church?"

Do some research about your area. Demographic information can be obtained from the last census. This often can found at the local library, by calling the Southern Baptist North American Mission Board (formerly Home Mission Board) in Alpharetta, Georgia, or by contacting your state convention or local association. You will be amazed at how much you can learn about the people who live near your church. This information will help you immensely in making strategic plans to reach the unsaved and unchurched.

While you are making pastoral calls, take an extra half hour to explore a part of the town (or rural area) where you have not been before. What kind of houses are in a particular area? How old are they? Are new ones being build? You also will want to familiarize yourself with the places where people work. Where do most of your church members live? Are they like the people you are trying to reach? Where are the most unreached people concentrated? You don't have to know all these answers the first month of your ministry. Learn as you go. The more you know about your community, the more you will feel a part of it.

Build your relationship with the unsaved and unchurched.— Set aside time each week (perhaps the church's weekly visitation time) to get to know and share a witness with the unsaved and unchurched. This will do more to keep you focused on your mission and purpose than anything you can do.

Build your relationship with the not-so-active members.—Ask someone (the Sunday School director, outreach leader, or church secretary) to give you the names, addresses, and phone numbers of four or five families who are attending church very little if any but who might be reclaimed. Visit them. This early point in your ministry is the best time to reach them. They cannot feel or say you have neglected them. You will reclaim some of them, and you will learn much about your church (some positive and some negative things). Put whatever you learn into perspective by realizing that their lack of commitment and sometimes guilt may affect what they say. Don't be defensive. Listening and caring will go a long way.

Build your relationship with shut-in members.—Some of the churches where I have served had a large number of shut-ins. Obviously, I could not call on any one individual often. This often is the case. If your church does not have a Homebound Department, an active deacon family ministry, or some other organizational structure that ministers to these important persons, express concern and ask for help. Along the way, this can be a ministry opportunity that the church can begin to meet. In the meantime, ask for the names of a few individuals you can call on. This is biblical ministry and creates a tremendous network of affirmation and support. You won't have to tell anybody that you made these calls. Those you have visited will tell everybody, and they will think their new pastor is wonderful.

For the first few months after I arrived at Central Baptist Church in Corbin, Kentucky, I blocked off about an hour one afternoon a week and would ask the church secretary to call about three shut-ins for appointment visits. Many of the homes were close enough that I could walk. (You can't do that everywhere.) You cannot imagine how many positive results came from being seen making those visits as well as from the visits themselves.

Build your relationship with nonmembers and a nonleadership group in the church.—You need to have contact with persons who are not members of your church. You also need to have contact with persons who are not leaders in your church. These contacts may come through some personal interest you have. My contacts have revolved around sports and my children. By playing on the church softball and basketball teams, I have kept in touch with people who are just being themselves and forget they are playing beside the preacher. I have had opportunities to reactivate inactive members, to stand at second base and share the gospel friend-to-friend, and to develop some of my strongest friendship. By attending events involving my children, I have sat with other parents who were there with their children. Some of these were church members and some were new friends who were reachable for Christ. You ought to attend these events with your children anyway, but attending will present opportunities for you to make yourself available to people and to make new friends. God can use you in these settings to open new doors for a positive Christian witness.

Open Your Door.

I am a strong advocate of an "open door" policy. Unless praying, deep in study, or involved in pastoral discussion with a person in need, I have made it my policy through the years, literally and figuratively, to keep my door open. The pastor needs to be accessible to the people. Far more complaints can be defused if you are approachable than if complainers are further frustrated by not being able to express their concerns to the pastor. Listen to people. Don't become defensive. On the other hand, don't believe you can solve every problem; and don't make promises that you may not be able to keep. Learn to say, "I'm sorry." You can be genuinely sorry they are disappointed or hurt without accepting blame. For most people, simply being able to tell their story is enough.

By leaving you door open, members often will drop by to share good news, to receive a word of encouragement, or to ask for prayer. These occasions build your ministry and leadership potential. You soon will learn the chronic complainers. When they come in, stand up, greet them, listen briefly. Then with a smile and a handshake or other appropriate action you can make the visit a short one. Even with chronic complainers and people with problems far beyond your training and expertise, being accessible to the people still is important. You even can say to the congregation, "I'll be available at the office. I'll pray for you in times of need. Feel free to call me at home in times of emergency. When you call me at home, I'll know you have a serious need. When that's the case, feel free to call me." This lets the congregation know that you are available, but it also reminds them that you should not be called about trivial matters when you are at home with your family.

A purpose statement is a concise wording of what your church is to do.

Focus You Attention.
While you are learning your church, study its purpose statement. Does your church have a purpose statement? If so, does it adequately define your church's mission that God has given it? If not, begin to talk with your leaders—Church Council, deacons, and other leadership groups—about the mission and purpose of the church. After planting the idea, convene an appropriate work group and begin to formulate a vision statement. This project can best be done during the early days of your ministry. This allows for maximizing the "honeymoon" effect of a new ministry.

As you focus attention on the church's purpose statement, revisit with church leaders or perhaps the whole congregation the Great Commission, the five functions of a church, and the four results of a healthy, growing church. Dr. Gene Mims' book, *Kingdom Principles for Church Growth*, clearly describes these functions and results.

A purpose statement is a concise wording of what your church is to do. The statement helps to clarify and focus the congregation's energies, gifts, programs, calendar, and budget on accomplishing what you believe God has in mind for your church. Some helpful steps toward a purpose can be:

Begin with a vision.—You are beginning the process of learning your church and community; you are building relationships. Now, what is the purpose of all this? What vision has God given you for your church and its role in building His kingdom? What vision has God given the people, especially the church leaders? How do you know? Ask them. Gather a church leadership group together and begin to pray and seek God's will. Talk about what the church is. Ask, "What are its strengths and weakness? What are its opportunities in the kingdom? What are the threats to its life and growth? What kinds of ministry gifts has God given individual members?" (At some point, you may want to do a more formal study of ministry gifts and lead your people to take a ministry gifts inventory, but for now you may want to explore those gifts through personal observation.) Ask, "What is going on in the church's community? Where do the people live? Where do they work? What is the demographic makeup of the community?" Ask the people to share the names of friends, family, and acquaintances who live within reach of your church. Share your vision, but especially guide the leadership group in sharing their visions.

Study the Great Commission.—Ask, What did Jesus mean by what He said in the Great Commission? How does it apply to our church? As you go through this process, remember that it is the Great Commission, not the great suggestion. A church does not have the option of rewriting the Great Commission. Its only option is to obey or to disobey its Lord's command. The leadership group's willingness to meet and to study the Great Commission indicates a desire to obey the Commission. Now, how can you and they move forward in obedience?

A church does not have the option of rewriting the Great Commission. Its only option is to obey or to disobey its Lord's command.

Write a purpose statement.—This simply is a prayed-over, hammered-out practical restatement of the Great Commission in the language of your congregation. The terms *purpose statement* and *vision statement* are used interchangeably. Precise terminology is not that important; but the statement, by whatever name it's called, must be consistent with the Great Commission. This concise statement (it should be easy to remember and state) is to become the driving force for the congregation. Take it to the church for discussion and adoption. Communicate it to the congregation from the pulpit and in church publications. Begin using it in planning sessions.

Kingdom Principles Growth Strategies, available from the Customer Service Center of the Baptist Sunday School Board, gives some excellent examples of vision or purpose statements on page 12. One of those examples states: "Our church will fulfill our Lord's command to reach, baptize, and teach those in our community by the power and presence of the Holy Spirit." Another example is, "Our church will fulfill the Great Commission by sharing the love of God in Christ with every person through evangelism, discipleship, ministry, fellowship, and worship." Do not simply adopt one of these example statements. Take the time to pray, discuss, and develop you own vision statement Your purpose statement needs to be your purpose statement.

Summary
You cannot immediately do all of the things suggested in this chapter. My prayer is that these suggestions (many of them have come out of my own pastoral experience) will help you begin a journey that will be used of God to build His kingdom, to bless your church, and to bring great joy to you and your family.

What kind of vision has God given you? Remember, "where there is no vision the people perish" (Prov. 29:8). The opposite also is true: "Where there is a vision the people flourish." It was so in the New Testament era, and it is so today.

---

[1] Michael D. Miller, *Kingdom Leadership*, (Nashville: Convention Press, 1996), 11.
[2] *The Minister's Family* (January-March, 1997), 1.

30

CHAPTER 2

Power to Go the Distance

● ●

"Turn again our captivity, O Lord, as the streams in the south" (Ps. 126:4).

The psalmist was wise enough to realize that the blessings of yesterday are not adequate for today. He asked God to pour out on Israel such a blessing that it would be like the down-pouring rains of the wet season that turned the parched, dry streams beds of the desert into rushing rivers. The singer was praying, as many of us are today, for a genuine spiritual revival, a true biblical awakening. When we begin to pray earnestly, passionately, and sincerely for such an awakening, we are on the way to becoming useful to our Lord.

Whether a general awakening sweeps across the land during your tenure in your present church and in your ministry, God wants to use you to grow His kingdom. That growth may be more like the working of leaven in flour or the development of a mustard seed than an "evangelism explosion." Even so, if you are where God has put you, stay there; be faithful; and be used of Him in His own way.

Be a Praying Pastor

As a kingdom leader, you have an awesome responsibility and a tremendous privilege. You have been given a God-sized task. You are under the burden of His call. The only possible way for you to meet that responsibility, fulfill that call, and have a long and fruitful ministry in your church and life is for you to be filled with the Holy Spirit and to be found in the will of God. Organization, administration, programs, and promotion are vital in channeling the Spirit's energies in your church. However, neither organization, administration, programs, nor promotion will be successful without the Spirit's power and without being founded and focused in God's will. The things of God can never be accomplished in human strength and ingenuity alone.

Neither organization, administration, programs, nor promotion will be successful without the Spirit's power.

Therefore, if you plan to have a long and fruitful ministry in God's kingdom and in your church, seek the infusion of the Holy Spirit and the will of God in prayer. Truly, the first and most important step in leading your church in kingdom growth is to determine God's will in everything you do. You do not need to pray to determine if it's God's will that the church and kingdom grow; the Scriptures make that truth abundantly clear. What you need to do is to pray that God will reveal to you His plan for how you are to be involved in that growth. Do not be guilty of formulating plans and then asking God to bless the plans that you already have made. Rather, as you review what God has shown you about your church and community, seek His wisdom so that you can know what plans to develop and use, and how plans others have developed and used successfully are to be adapted to your life and your church.

A huge difference exists between wisdom and knowledge. Knowledge is information and skills. Wisdom is the ability to make right and good use of information and skills. Knowledge is knowing how;

wisdom is knowing what and when. Knowledge is having the technology to do great things; wisdom is knowing how to make the right decisions and choices to use the technology. We have an abundance of growth methods. We have multitudes of plans and programs. How do we chose from among them? Which plan, if any, do you use? Plans and programs are instruments (tools). They are of value only when they are used according to God's will. Only God-given wisdom can teach you how and when to use them. Pray for that wisdom. God promises, "If any of you lack wisdom, let him ask of God, that giveth to all men liberally, and upbraideth not; and it shall be given him" (Jas. 1:5).

Not only do we need God's wisdom to determine the right plans for each individual church's growth, we also need wisdom that will enable us to involve the right persons in this growth. These persons cannot be enlisted effectively by pleas, threats, or guilt trips. They can be enlisted only by sharing our God-given dreams and vision. Only as we can say enthusiastically and confidently, "This is the will of God for our church" can we expect others to be moved by the Holy Spirit to catch the vision and believe that God will give the harvest. Jesus told us to "pray ye therefore the Lord of the harvest, that he would send forth laborers into his harvest" (Luke 10:2). The harvest is God's, not ours. He must teach us how to sow, cultivate, and harvest. He must send forth the laborers, or they will be ineffective and will become disillusioned. God invites us to join Him in kingdom growth (1 Cor. 3:9). He will move upon the minds and hearts of His leaders through the Holy Spirit as they pray to call laborers into His harvest.

As you pray for growth, God will help you see where the ripe harvest is and will lead you to the tools that will be most effective in reaping the harvest. As you pray for plans and personnel to used in the harvest, God's tug on your heart will influence even the way you make announcements. Enthusiastic announcements and active support of a program by the kingdom leader often are the prime human elements in the program's success. I am convinced that the human element in the success of most programs is 90 percent enthusiasm, and the initial spark of that enthusiasm in the church must come from the pastor. What is true, biblical enthusiasm? The literal meaning of the word *enthusiasm* is "to be inbreathed or inspired by God." How can you be so inspired by God that you can lead and motivate others? Only through deep, persistent, Spirit-directed prayer.

An active devotional life is a must for all kingdom leaders. We must have times when we read the Bible and allow it to speak to us. We must avoid the preacher syndrome of always looking for a sermon text when we read the Bible. Of course, God wants to speak to us so that we can preach His message to others, but never forget that He also wants to speak to us because we personally need a word from Him. And, never forget that the Spirit speaks to us most clearly when we wait before Him in prayer with an open Bible and an open mind.

Lead Your Church to Be a Praying Church

The pastor is responsible for leading his church to be a praying church by practicing and teaching prayer and by leading his church in prayer. In prayer as at no other place, Jesus is the kingdom leader's role model. And, in prayer, more than in any other ministry, the pastor must be his church's role model.

Kingdom leadership, kingdom ministry, and kingdom preaching can never be separated from prayer in the God-called pastor's life and ministry. God has given him a message that makes an eternal difference in the lives of men, women, boys, and girls. His proclamation of that message must flow out of his prayer life.

Practice Prayer in Your Own Life

We can only imagine the burden Jesus carried as He walked through the darkness from the upper room to Gethsemane. John 17 gives us the privilege of listening in on the Savior's prayer as the shadow of the cross hung heavily over Him. First, Jesus prayed that all the final events of His life on earth would bring honor and glory to His Father (vv. 1–8). Then He prayed that His immediate followers would be empowered to carry on His work after His departure (vv. 9–19). Jesus did not pray that those disciples would be taken out of the world. He prayed that they would be kept by the Father as they did the work Jesus had given them to do. Finally, Jesus prayed for us—those who would be saved down though the ages through the preaching of the gospel and those who would be called out to special kingdom service through the Holy Spirit (vv. 20–26).

Jesus' prayer recorded in John 17 is the perfect model of a kingdom leader's prayer and one every pastor would do well to emulate. Pray for yourself. The devil would like very much for you to destroy your witness through immorality, dishonesty, deceit, or things as simple as frustration and anger. Pray daily that God will keep you pure, deeply in love with the Savior, zealous in your ministry, and compassionate toward people. Pray for the witness and the needs of the people you lead. They are as human as you are and desperately in need of the power of Christ to live the gospel in their world of school, business, home, and leisure time. Pray for those who lead the nations of the world. Pray for God's worldwide mission program and for missionaries by name. Pray for the unsaved and for all people everywhere. Do not leave anyone out of your prayer life.

Pray for all of God's churches, even your next-door neighbor. Sometimes it is more difficult to pray for the growth and success of the church down the road whose methods are different from yours and whose leadership personalities are hard to like. But remember, God is building His kingdom by using all of His children. Often a real test of our prayer life is whether we can pray that God will use us in leading to salvation those who will not join our church; or that God will lead persons out of our church to other places of service after we've invested so much in discipling them. But that is kingdom praying. It is the way Jesus prayed and the way He would have us pray. Many of us have seen God bless in the long-term, often in unexpected ways, in our own ministries when we have been faithful in practicing kingdom leadership and kingdom praying. Dr. Michael D. Miller has an excellent chapter entitled "Jesus Christ: The Leader and Spiritual Conflict" in his book *Kingdom Leadership* that you might find very helpful as a prayer resource.

Teach Your Church to Pray

As God's called servant-leader, you have a responsibility to teach your congregation to pray. The Bible contains so many scriptural patterns for teaching prayer, but the clearest model is Jesus Himself. In learning to pray, two questions must be answered: How to pray, and what to pray for? Both questions are answered by Jesus in the Model Prayer of Matthew 6:5–15. Jesus gave His disciples the spiritual conditions and the specific content of prayer.

He taught them to pray sincerely (vv. 5–6).—This is the first prerequisite of prayer. Jesus did not condemn public prayer; He condemned praying to impress an audience. The question is motive, not place. We need to make sure that we pray with the right attitude and right motives. We need to ask, "Is my prayer a performance, or is it pure?"

Real prayer is to talk with and listen to God as you would talk with your best friend. If we love someone, we want to spend time with him or her. Jesus did not mean that we are never to pray in public; but if we pray only in public before an admiring audience, we are hypocrites. We are to pray privately and publicly, but Jesus emphasized private prayer. Indeed, we pray better publicly if we pray privately. And, we pray better privately if we are not ashamed of the Savior publicly.

He taught them to pray simply (vv. 7–8).—Jesus did not condemn constantly and continuously praying for the same needs until God meets those needs according to His will. Jesus condemned meaningless repetition—babbling or rambling on and on in a torrent of words—that had as its purpose to pressure God into acting. We should never interpret this passage to mean that we are to pray once or twice and forget it. Indeed, the apostle Paul urged us to "[continue] instant in prayer" (Rom. 12:12).

We pray better publicly, if we pray privately. And, we pray better privately, if we are not ashamed of the Savior publicly.

Other Scriptures show that continuous, persistent prayer is not meaningless. In two parables on prayer (Luke 11:5–9; 18:1–8), Jesus emphasized persistence in prayer. Even He repeated His petition when He prayed in Gethsemane. Repetition caused by a burdened heart is not meaningless. Times come when our prayer burden is so intense that we can't help but repeatedly cry out to our heavenly Father (Jas. 4:2–3). We are not to try to "plea bargain" with God or to make deals with Him. We are to pray clearly, specifically, confidently, consistently, and in the will of God. We are to seek to discover what He wants us to do and what He wants to do through us.

He taught them to pray specifically (vv. 9–13).—Jesus instructed us to pray for our needs as well as the needs of others. He encouraged us to pray about the simplest things in life as well as the more crucial needs. In the Model Prayer, Jesus taught us to pray for our daily bread. Bread represents the basic necessities of life. Whatever we need, God is willing to provide if we ask. We are dependent on Him to supply our needs, and He wants to do so out of His abundance (Phil. 4:19). The Father surely knows we need bread, but what a difference it makes in our prayer life when we understand that God does not have to be convinced of our needs or argued into answering our prayers.

More than anything else, we need forgiveness. Sincerely praying for forgiveness requires that our hearts be free of malice toward others (vv. 14–15). We also are to pray that God will deliver us from temptation and from Satan.

Real prayer begins with a recognition of God as Father and closes with an affirmation of God as Sovereign Ruler. The Father is willing to hear us. The Sovereign Ruler of the universe is abundantly more than able to supply our needs.

We need to be taught and to teach others how to pray. We have no power apart from God's power. Perhaps more than His power, we need His presence. No better model could be used in teaching our people to pray than the model given by Jesus Himself. Jesus taught us to agree with one another in prayer (Matt. 18:19–20). Over and over again in the Book of Acts we find the church praying together and God answering in power (Acts 12:5). Paul commanded the church at Thessalonica to "pray without ceasing" (1 Thess. 5:17). Twice Paul asked that same church to "pray for us" (1 Thess. 5:25; 2 Thess. 3:1). James 5:13–16 gives the church specific instructions about prayer. From a practical standpoint, church members learn more about prayer from example than from any other form of teaching.

Lead the Church in Prayer
Pastors will lead the church to pray on many occasions and will use many methods. Here are a few suggested occasions.

Pray on Sunday morning.—The congregation needs to hear the pastor pray during the worship service. Prayer is a relationship, not just religious activity. In that relationship, get in tune with the

Holy Spirit and express to God your concerns and those of the congregation by leading them in prayer.

Pray about specific needs and specific persons during Sunday morning worship. Mention members and attendees of the church who are sick or in the hospital, but don't fall into the trap of mentioning every possible need of friends and distant relatives of church members or of mentioning details of the needs. Just pray for the persons. Some needs should not be mentioned, and a lengthy prayer list can distract from the prayer time and consume the worship service. You may want to ask the person or family ahead of time whether a particular person would want their name mentioned. I have discovered that mentioning lost persons by name on Sunday morning is not wise. You may embarrass them or their families and destroy the possibility of winning that person or family to Christ. By all means, be careful about asking the congregation to mention prayer needs during the worship service unless you are prepared to have a good deal of your worship time taken up with this activity. However, people often desperately want the church's prayers for a critical need, and you may want to devise a system such as a tear-off tab on the worship bulletin or prayer needs cards in the pews for them to turn in their prayer needs. Occasionally remind the congregation of the ground rules you follow in prayer during the Sunday morning worship service, and use discretion.

Involve the congregation in prayer times. While head are bowed and eyes are closed, you may want to ask the congregation to raise their hands, if they are praying for a lost person, a need in their own life or someone else's, or a particular church concern. Generally, it's best to ask various persons in the congregation to lead in prayer, not just the pastor, staff, deacons, or "important" church members. Be sure to ask permission before you call on someone to lead in prayer. You may want to enlist persons ahead of time to lead in prayer, and you may want to list their names in the worship bulletin. Mention to the congregation that you have asked the person ahead of time to lead in prayer. Some great and godly people are not comfortable leading in public prayer, and some persons have become less active in church or have dropped out altogether because they were afraid of being called on to lead in prayer. Although schedules are tight and time is precious, make sure nothing crowds out appropriate prayer time on Sunday morning.

Pray on Sunday evening.—Much of what has been said about Sunday morning applies to the Sunday evening service. But typically, more time for sharing is available on Sunday evening. This is the time you may want to ask the congregation to share briefly their prayer needs. The evening service with its closeness and unity may afford occasions for an "altar of prayer" invitation, especially if the church is facing a significant need or event—a revival, a pastoral or staff change, a time of sorrow or burden about a particular need, or similar occasions.

Pray on Wednesday evening.—For many of our churches midweek prayer service offers opportunities for congregational and small-group times of extensive and intensive prayer. The church should keep an active prayer needs list. In a smaller church, a trusted volunteer often can be enlisted to write down the names and needs that are mentioned by the congregation. Encourage that person to keep the list up-to-date. Ask worshipers not only to add new names and needs to the prayer list but to up-date the list and to remove names and needs that no longer should be on the list. The removal of names may be an occasion of special prayer for their families such as when a sick person has passed away. Or, God may have given healing or solved the problem. Don't forget to have a time for praise. An active, current prayer needs list helps make congregational prayer times more meaningful.

Wednesday night can be a time for using a variety of prayer methods. Here are some ideas: Have the people gather by twos or in larger groups and take turns praying aloud. Read the prayer needs one at a time, and let the people pray for each need silently. Use the church altar. Assign the pews to individuals, and have one or more persons kneel at every pew and pray for those who will be in those pews on Sunday morning. The variety of prayer methods is unlimited, and prayer is indispensable.

Pray at special times.—Look for special times and special ways to emphasis prayer. Make much of special times and weeks of prayer. Support special days of prayer. Support youth and others who "meet at the pole" and at other times to pray with the larger Christian community. You may want to encourage prayer chains, prayer teams, or prayer intercessor meetings in a separate room while the worship service is being conducted.

Ask God to show you ways to encourage and to practice prayer. Pray, using every appropriate means. Look for new ways to focus on prayer. For many years I have used one-minute and five-minute spots on radio to share a verse of Scripture, a thought, and a prayer. These are effective, especially on secular radio. In a one-minute spot you can speak to an audience that will not be in church on Sunday, especially if the spot is placed between two songs, near the news, or during a sports event.

Dial-a-devotion ministry has been very effective in my ministry. All this ministry takes is a phone line (an easy-to-remember number helps), an answering machine, inexpensive tapes, and a willingness to spend a little time. You can read a verse of Scripture, share a few thoughts, and pray for the person who is listening. It's amazing how personal the ministry can be. (Don't address the caller as "he" or "she." You don't know who is calling. Address them as "the one who is calling" or "you." Also don't say "today" or "tonight." People will call at all hours. Say "right now.") Dial-a-devotions will take a little time, but the time will be well spent.

Pray without ceasing. Teach the people to pray everyday, all the time. And remember, prayer is the key to the power a pastor or any other minister needs to help him over the long haul.

CHAPTER 3

Preaching That Endures

• •

People still come to church to hear a word from the Lord. Once God has called you to preach, the question no longer is "Do I preach?" The question is "How and what do I preach?" The sermon is not the only preaching that occurs during a worship service. Enthusiastic singing and other celebrative music, sincere praying, relevant drama, and an enthusiastic biblical message all presented in a fashion to enhance worship are at the heart of the functions of a church. Surely, the kingdom leader is compelled to agonize over every aspect of preparing for and leading public worship.

The church that is concerned about kingdom growth is interested not only in those who are now in attendance but those who are prospects. Therefore, we must do everything possible to reduce the "intimidation factors" of our services without compromising the message. The church building intimidates. It represents a holy God, and persons without Christ are keenly aware of their unworthiness to approach Him. The unknowns behind the doors of our churches are frightening to the unsaved and unchurched. Our problem is, how can we make the worship services of our churches more inviting to the unsaved and unchurched? More importantly, how can you as a pastor of the gospel give leadership that insures that every element of the service revolves around the message God wants conveyed? How can you insure that your message speaks to real human needs?

Whatever else pastors do, their primary responsibility is to preach the Bible.

Pastors are torn in a variety of directions by demanding schedules. They have a huge variety of tasks, but whatever else they do, their primary responsibility is to preach the Bible. Their responsibility is to pray and prepare so that when the people arrive, their pastor will have a word for them from God. The Bible is relevant. True preaching with exposition, illustration, and application to life always will meet human needs.

The pastor's preaching style affects the entire church. If you are prepared, the church comes to feel that the message of the Bible is important. If you preach enthusiastically, hearers will get excited about God's message and God's work. If you apply the Scriptures to human needs, the people look to the Bible for answers. Preaching changes lives. Preaching is a privilege. If the preacher really believes and preaches the Bible, the Sunday School teachers will believe the Bible, the members will read the Bible, witnesses will share the message of the Bible, and the church will become a people of the Bible. What the preacher preaches is of ultimate importance. How could those of us who preach the Bible not agonize under the burden of preaching?

The burden of preaching does not mean that it is not a joy. If you have been called to preach, you can use humor, drama, dialogue, and scores of innovations to communicate the gospel. What could be a greater joy for the God-called preacher than preaching? Keep that joy and excitement in your life through prayer and Bible study and by celebrating the preaching event each time you preach.

Preaching is at the heart of evangelism. When you preach, if you really believe that individuals without Christ are lost and without hope, the inviting and exciting message of salvation will come through. Your message of the kingdom will challenge the church to reach out. No other person has the ear of the people like the pastor. A growing church inevitably has a pastor who is so committed to growth that when he opens his mouth he preaches growth convictions, ideas, and plans. Preach church and kingdom growth. Jesus preached growth. He promised, "I will build my church" (Matt. 16:18). In the Great Commission, Jesus challenges us to go and to make disciples of all nations, and He promises to empower us as we go. He said, "Lift up your eyes, and look on the fields; for they are white already to harvest" (John 4:35). Remember, Jesus is our model for everything, including preaching.

Preaching is absolutely vital for the God-called pastor. God has given him a message that makes an eternal difference in the lives of men, women, boys, and girls.

How do I deliver that life-changing message? Are preaching methods important? What is the best way to preach God's message effectively? Do style and delivery make a difference? Some surveys tend to show that preaching styles and even quality of preaching are less important than the burning heart of the preacher in imparting a vision and communicating a sense of urgency out of which growth will occur.[1] This should not surprise us since preaching provides the platform for motivation and maintaining a healthy, celebrative spirit. Even so, I am still convinced that preaching style makes a difference in church growth, especially in the congregation's spiritual growth.

Experience has shown me that expository preaching is the best all-round preaching style, and my advice to any preacher is, preach expository sermons. Can a church grow from preaching that is not primarily expository? Absolutely! God has blessed my pastoral ministry with two unusual experiences of spiritual and numerical church growth. The first occurred at Southside Baptist Church in Princeton, Kentucky, a town of 6,500 people. My ministry there began with a Sunday School attendance of 125 and a worship attendance of 150. Over the 11 years of my service with the church, attendance in Sunday School grew to 350 with 450 in worship services. During those years my Sunday preaching was almost exclusively topical except for an occasional textual sermon. I sometimes did a homily on Wednesday evening. Homilies are not to be confused with expository sermons. Homilies simply give a running commentary on a Bible passage.

As I moved along in my ministry, I began listening to tapes by outstanding expository preachers. I became convinced that expository preaching was better. During the latter months of my ministry with Southside, I began to experiment with various preaching styles. I soon made a commitment to myself to become an expository preacher. This new conviction coincided with a move to a new pastorate. From the beginning of my ministry with Central Baptist Church, Corbin, Kentucky, I preached expository sermons almost exclusively. My practice was to preach through books of the Bible. In larger books, I did not preach from every verse. I preached from chapters or sections. In shorter books, I often preached verse by verse. My ministry in Corbin began with an attendance of about 330 in Sunday School and about 400 in worship. In this town of 7,700, attendance grew to average 950 in Sunday School and about 1,100 in worship.

The principle thing about preaching is that it be thoroughly biblical.

Does expository preaching cause church growth or the lack of expository preaching prevent church growth? No. The principle things about preaching are that it be thoroughly biblical, that it speaks to the people's needs, and that it conveys God's message to the people. A wise pastor will teach his congregation to bring their Bibles and to use them in the worship services—and in their lives.

The advantages of expository preaching are many. This preaching style corresponds to the biblical pattern of preaching and to the way the Bible was written. The Bible was written sentence by sentence, paragraph by paragraph, and the books were written as wholes. As we have it, the Bible is in a verse by verse, chapter by chapter arrangement. Preaching the Bible as it was written meets every conceivable spiritual need and makes for a well-instructed people. It tends to keep a healthy balance in preaching and keeps the preacher off of his favorite sermon hobby horse. This does not mean that the preacher should become a slave to expository preaching. Variety in preaching style is good, but inevitably preachers find themselves developing certain preaching patterns and relying more heavily on one style than others.

My use of expository preaching style grew out of my convictions. Make sure your preferred preaching style grows out of your heartfelt convictions, not out of the line of least resistance. Topical sermons are easiest to prepare, but are they best for a steady preaching diet for the people? Make sure you are the kind of preacher that God intended for you to be when He called you. If I had my ministry to do over, would I change anything about my preaching? Yes, from day one I would become an expository preacher. I believe that is the best way to preach all the Word of God. Will God bless other preaching styles? Of course! He will bless any sermon that is thoroughly biblical and preached with sincerity and enthusiasm. In fact, God sometimes blesses even when some desirable preaching ingredients are missing. Remember, God promises to bless His Word, not our words. He says, "So shall My word be that goes forth from My mouth; it shall not return to Me void, but it shall accomplish what I please, and it shall prosper in the thing for which I sent it" (Isa. 55:11, NKJV).[2]

Mix in some topical, textual, dramatic, and narrative sermons along with your expository preaching. Some sermons such as doctrinal or life-needs sermons lend themselves to topical or textual preaching. Narrative and story sermons can convey a great deal of biblical information and forcefully drive home a particular point. Drama can, in a disarming way, communicate a very pointed, effective message. When used appropriately, all these preaching styles can supplement a steady diet of expository preaching and can create a very interesting and enjoyable sermon menu for the listeners and the preacher.

Expository preaching prevents the preacher from wasting his time searching for a text or an idea to preach, and it makes for a well-instructed congregation. It also forces the preacher to study and to prepare well. The discipline of this kind of Bible study will keep the preacher spiritually fresh and growing. It also will help in planning a preaching calendar. Put the calendar and the Bible side by side. To your amazement, you will find that even special holidays will be well provided for by passages from within the book from which you are preaching. Sometimes you may want to preach from a text to fit a particular occasion that is ahead of or behind where you have been preaching, but even this allows continuity within a given Bible book. Expository preaching also maximizes study resources and the use of your study time. For example, if the Spirit impresses you to preach through the Book of Nehemiah in preparation for a future building program, you can begin gathering commentaries and start a general study of the book long before you begin to preach through it.

Expository preaching will force you to preach on passages and to address particular needs that probably neither you nor the congregation would choose for a sermon. But, just as your physical body needs certain vitamins whether the need is felt or not, individuals and the church need certain subjects addressed whether they are aware of it or not. Sooner or later, right on God's schedule, the Bible will speak to every spiritual need.

Another advantage of preaching through a Bible book is that when the preacher addresses a sensitive subject, people will not be inclined to think, *Well, wonder who's guilty of that?* or *What's going on that we don't know about?* Further, as you speak to the life needs of the people through declaration, exposition, illustration, and application, you produce an increasing hunger and love for the Scriptures and God's message.

How many sermons should be preached from a given Bible book? That depends on the length of the book, the congregation's needs, and the preacher's personality. Too few sermons from a book may treat it superficially; too many may produce boredom. I preached 54 sermons from Acts, 36 from John, 12 from Nehemiah, 16 from the Epistles of John, 15 from Philippians, and 13 from James. In most cases, I preached straight through a book— Sunday morning, Sunday evening, and Wednesday night.

Every verse of a Bible book may not be read publicly, but it is a good practice to preach from virtually every chapter and most of the major events and themes. Preaching straight through a book in consecutive services communicates that Sunday evenings and Wednesday evenings are important, and attendance often will increase.

Some passages within most books lend themselves to being better treated with a teaching homily rather than an expository sermon, and some verses can best be treated textually. The needs of the various services and prayerful scheduling allow you to plan your preaching to match passages to the various kinds of services and congregational needs.

One further word about preaching methods and styles: Do not become a slave to any particular sermon style. I agree with the statement I heard a country preacher make some years ago: "Don't let your homiletics get in the way of your preaching." You may preach a sermon that doesn't fit any definable pattern. It might have gotten a D-minus from a homiletics professor; but if four people got saved, I'd say that God gave it an A+, wouldn't you? So give God the praise and keep on preaching!

Be ready to respond spontaneously to the momentary leadership of the Holy Spirit.

Preach extemporaneously.—The sermon needs to be well prepared and outlined (many preachers find that alliteration makes it easy for them and people to remember the outline), but your sermon delivery should not be bound by what is written on paper. Be open to the unexpected. Be ready to respond spontaneously to the momentary leadership of the Holy Spirit. This is not an argument for preaching without notes and certainly not for unpreparedness. It is an argument for being so well prepared that you are free in your delivery. Again, many great preachers literally have read their sermons word for word from manuscripts; and if that best fits your gifts, use what God has given you. If you are comfortable in preaching without an outline, preach that way for the glory of God. However, for many of us, at least a skeleton outline is very useful. Even so, we do not want to be bound by it

Preach enthusiastically.—Get excited about your message! Look for various and unique ways to invite people to Christ through your sermons. Seek opportunities through the text with application and illustration to motivate your people to do evangelism. Urge evangelism repeatedly. Remember, the primary factor in motivation is enthusiasm, and true godly enthusiasm is the flow of the Holy Spirit through the preacher. Study and pray. Pray and study. Keep doing these until your preaching is enthusiastic. If your preaching already is enthusiastic, don't take it for granted. Keep on praying and studying! Enthusiastic preaching can be enhanced by attention to details in preparation.

Use a variety of introductions.—So much of the effectiveness of a sermon depends on capturing the congregation's attention. This can be done by a well-prepared introduction. You may introduce the sermon by giving the biblical context, defining your subject, focusing on a special occasion, referring to a current event, reciting a striking quotation, or using an illustration or a funny story. Do not fall into the routine of constantly using the same kind of introduction, especially if you are preaching to the same congregation week after week.

Apply the sermon.—Placing the text in its historical setting is important, but don't leave your message in yesterday. Consider three questions: What did the Scripture mean in its historical setting? What does it mean today? And, what does it mean to this congregation? Answer these questions as you preach the message to your congregation. Virtually every point of the sermon ought to answer one of the first two questions, and every point of a true sermon needs to deal with the third question.

Use illustrations wisely.—We live in a picture-conscious world. I often have talked with someone who remembered a story I had told years earlier. They did not remember much else about the sermon, but they remembered the story and the application. Properly told, tasteful stories attract attention and kindle an emotional response to the sermon. Good illustrations are like windows in the sermon: They help your listeners say, "Oh, I see." They are like little sparks that jolt your congregation's attention.

Humorous illustrations often can be used to relax your congregation and to draw them back when their minds have wandered away. Remember, however, that humor can poke fun at something or someone. Be careful not to use illustrations that reflect negatively on someone or some ethnic or culture group. It's always safe to make yourself the target of your humorous illustrations. If you tell a humorous story about a member or family of your congregation, be sure you have their permission to do so. Otherwise, you may cause resentment in that person or family and their friends. Never embarrass your congregation with off-color jokes and language. Don't try to clean up an off-color joke and make it useable in the pulpit. You may have someone in your congregation who has heard the seamier version and will know what you have done. Use good, tasteful humor, but don't appear to be a stand-up comic. You are God's preacher delivering God's message. If humor helps you do that, well; if not, forget it.

Make your illustrations believable. Get the facts straight in your illustrations, and be sure your sources are reliable. Few things are more disturbing to a congregation than hearing their pastor relate inaccurate information in a sermon. Don't say an incident happened to you unless it did. You may have someone in your audience who has heard two or three other preachers tell that the same incident happened to them. If that happens, you call into question your integrity and the validity of your sermon.

Another caution: Do not overuse illustrations. Don't let your sermon become a string of stories stuck together with a little verbal glue. Don't let your illustrations get too long and distract the congregation from the heart of your sermon. Illustrations are instruments to communicate the Word of God, so don't use them for their own sake. Sometimes you will have a good story you are itching to tell. Rein yourself in and ask, "Does this great story fit and enhance the sermon, or do I just want to tell it because it's a good story?"

One of the best methods for illustrating and communicating the sermon is through drama. Part or all of your sermon may be drama. You may do the drama yourself, or other persons may help introduce or apply the sermon through drama. The use of drama in preaching is very effective today. Most churches have persons who are gifted and interested in drama. Encourage them to develop various presentations that can tastefully and powerfully illustrate a sermon. Youth often are interested in drama and can communicate in a powerful way messages that deal with a wide variety of biblical passages.

Give a creative, appealing invitation.—Simply and clearly invite persons to respond to Christ. Tell them what you want them to do as a result of the sermon, and invite them to do it. Crystallize what you have said, especially in the last point of the sermon. Invitation time is time to be personal. Talk directly, conversationally, and personally to the people. Make each person feel that the message has been addressed personally to him or her and to no one else. The use of personal pronouns—*you, your, we, us, our, ours*—gives your message a direct, warm, personal touch. Let the invitation ride the crest of the sermon's emotional climax. Allow the congregation to feel that their response to God's message will make a difference.

Give the invitation, expecting people to respond. Do not browbeat them or use humor in the invitation. It is not appropriate here. Don't drag out the invitation or re-preach your sermon, but give the people time to respond without being rushed. If the response is not what you had hoped and prayed it would be, don't let your discouragement show, and don't become hostile. Commit the service to God. Believe that He will do His work. You may want to remind the people that you are available to speak with them after the close of the service or later in the week, and invite them to give you a call.

As you close the service, begin to get ready in your heart for the next message God is going to give you. Believe that He will use it. Indeed, He will. God's ministry is the world's most important work. Pray and preach; preach and pray. They are inseparable in the life of the man of God called to agonize over a lost world for whom Christ died. Let God's message be to you like His message was to Jeremiah: "His word was in my heart like a burning fire shut up in my bones; I was weary of holding it back, and I could not" (Jer. 20:9, NKJV).

---

[1] See C. Kirk Hadaway, *Church Growth Principles* (Nashville: Broadman Press, 1991).
[2] From the *New King James Version.* Copyright © 1979, 1980, 1982, Thomas Nelson, Inc., Publishers.

CHAPTER 4

Leadership That Lasts

· ·

*"He that goeth forth and weepeth, bearing
precious seed, shall doubtless come again with
rejoicing, bringing his sheaves with him"*
                                        (Ps 126:6).

Kingdom service is very, very personal. Notice the psalmist's
use of the personal pronouns *he, his,* and *him*. The inspired songwriter placed the emphasis on personal involvement. Someone has to go forth. Someone has to do the weep-
ing, sowing, and reaping. Who is going to be used of the Lord?
You and me, if we are willing and useable, that's who.

An old deacon farmer gave his young pastor some sound advice. He said, "Son, you see all them stumps in that field out
there?" "Yes, sir," replied the young pastor. "Well, son,"

declared the old farmer, "I can spend the whole summer digging up stumps and losing my crop, or I can plow around the stumps and save my crop. Son, the same is true in your ministry here. You can spend all your time digging up the stumps in this church, or you can plow around them and go on with your ministry. Son, my advice is to plow around them." And, that's good advice for every pastor.

The word *lead* implies being out in front. However, if the leader is so far out front that his followers cannot see clearly the way he is going or understand his leadership, they have difficulty following, even when they want to. If the leader's path and instructions are uncertain and erratic—if he goes first one way, then another, and still another—followers become confused and discouraged. If the leader gets behind his people and tries to drive them, they have no one out front showing the way to go. Some will go one way; others will go another; and some simply will stop. If the leader gets frustrated with his people and shouts at them, they become frightened and angry, and will scatter. If the leader mixes in with his people without any direction in his own life, they will lose respect for his leadership ability and will not follow.

The kingdom leader must be one of the group that he is seeking to lead and still be somewhat apart from them.

The kingdom leader must be one of the group that he is seeking to lead and still be somewhat apart from them. He must not lord it over them, yet he must know that he is the leader and speak with confidence. He must be out in front, but not too far; and he must communicate to his followers that he knows where he is going and what he is doing. The kingdom leader must model what he is trying to teach and where he is trying to lead the church, and he must do it in a relational style so that his followers will understand that they too can do the things they see their leader doing.

Describing a kingdom leader is difficult, but being one is even more difficult. Being a kingdom leader is not a science; it's an art. It's not a list of rules; it's a set of principles and a living spirit. Being a kingdom leader requires the Holy Spirit's supernatural power. Jesus promised this power to all believers. He said, "Verily, verily, I say unto you, He that believeth on me, the works that I do shall he do also; and greater works than these shall he do; because I go unto my Father" (John 14:12).

Kingdom leadership is personal. God uses persons to build His kingdom. What kind of persons? Persons with principles. What kind of principles? Kingdom principles like these.

Be Certain of Your Call

It's time to ask, Why are you in the ministry? If it's because you simply decided it would be a good vocation, get out! If it's because you have been trained in it, change vocations. If a beloved family member or dear personal friend "called" you into the ministry, confess your mistake; and begin to serve Jesus as a committed Christian layman. If, on the other hand, you can say, "I am in the ministry because the One who saved me called me into the ministry," stay. God will use you mightily in His kingdom. Also, be sure you can say, "The God who called me into the ministry called me to this particular place of ministry." This will cause you to "stay put" when things aren't going well. It will allow you to rejoice even when you cannot see victories you long for, and it will cause you to celebrate when God is blessing with visible victories.

Love the Lord

Can you say, "No one ever loved me like Jesus, and I love Him with all my heart; therefore, when He called, I answered with a lifelong 'yes' "? Following Jesus' resurrection, the Savior talked with Simon Peter by the Sea of Galilee. While Jesus was on trial for His life, Peter denied Him three times. Now the time had come to take inventory.

After Jesus had eaten breakfast with the disciples, the Lord turned to Peter and asked, "Lovest thou me?" Three times Jesus asked this question, changing His words slightly each time so that His questions became more and more personal. Peter replied, "Lord, Thou knowest all things; thou knowest that I love thee." Jesus replied, in effect, "Then show your love by giving your life to the ones I love" (John 21:15–17). Peter did exactly that. He spent the rest of his life serving Christ. He loved Jesus. Therefore, he loved the people Jesus loved.

More than anything else, your love for the Savior will shape your ministry. If that love is not warm, fresh, and alive, find a quiet place; open your Bible; open your heart; let God speak to you; renew your love for Him. Your ministry, your lifestyle, your courage, your leadership must flow out of your love for the Lord.

Love Your Church

If God has called you to your present place of ministry, you are right where you ought to be. Since these are the people God has given to you to lead, believe in your heart that these are the best people anywhere to whom and through whom you can minister. If you do not love your congregation, you have two honest choices—fall in love with them or move. Actually, the second choice is not a valid choice. If God has called you to that ministry location and wants you to stay, loving your people is your only genuine choice.

Loving your people means that you accept them for who and what they are and determine to do your best to lead them to where God wants them to be.

Loving your people does not mean that you love all their actions and attitudes. It means that you accept them for who and what they are and determine to do your best to lead them to where God wants them to be. Help God pick them up when they fall. In love, preach to them about their sins. Lead them in prayers of repentance. Help them to know that God forgives their sins, and be sure you forgive them. Brag on them when they do well. Rejoice with them when good things happen in their lives. Take time to listen to them. Ask about their families. Talk with them about areas of interest. Notice the special things that happen in their lives. Encourage them to be proud to be Christians and members of your church. Invite them to be on the team with their pastor. If you love them, they will know it and will follow you. If you don't love them, they will know it and will not follow you.

Years ago I had lunch with a staff member of a church in the mountains of Eastern Kentucky in the area where I was serving. Almost as soon as we sat down, he began to talk about the ignorance and backwardness of the area. For the rest of the meal, he constantly downgraded the people. He obviously felt deprived and slighted that he had to minister in that area. Before long, I found myself boiling on the inside. Although I'd been in the area only a few months, these were my people. Finally I said to him, "Since it's such a burden and sacrifice for you to be here, you ought to move. You might as well; you're not going to be effective." He was astonished. He couldn't understand what I meant. Are you surprised when I tell you that he had a short troubled ministry before being forced to resign?

Jesus the Great Shepherd set the example for His undershepherds. He said, "This is my commandment, That ye love one another, as I have loved you" (John 15:12). He also said, "The sheep hear his voice; and he calleth his own sheep by name, and leadeth them out. And when he putteth forth his own sheep, he goeth before them, and the sheep follow him: for they know his voice" (John 10:3–4).

When you love the people, they will love and trust you. They will open up to you and share their problems. Loving them takes time and involves headaches and heartaches, but it's worth it. Colin Powell said, "The day soldiers stop bringing you their problems is the day you have stopped leading them. They have either lost confidence that you can help them or concluded that you do not care. Either case is a failure of leadership."[1]

Practice What You Preach

The easy part of the ministry is preaching; the hard part is living out what we preach. Only Jesus practiced every word He uttered, but that is no excuse for us to tolerate on-going sins and failures in our lives. When we fail, we must be wise enough to confess our humanness. However, prevention of many failures is simply a matter of discipline. Surely, we would expect of ourselves what we expect of others.

Practice evangelism.—If you preach that the people should be involved in outreach visitation, be faithfully involved yourself and give leadership to outreach. Unless you are hindered by being in a pulpit preaching, miles away on a trip, genuinely sick, or such like, be present and be involved in evangelistic visitation, especially if you expect it of others. They may not be as faithful as you are, but they certainly are not going to more faithful than you.

Practice stewardship.—Tithe, whether you preach it or not (it's biblical), but especially if you preach it. Also, remember that a part of stewardship is proper handling of the resources the church provides. Be frugal with the church's money. Many people in the pews give sacrificially. Think of those people when you are spending the church's money. Whether you are traveling, purchasing material, or simply spending time, be a good steward.

Participate in worship.—When you encourage the people to worship during the worship services, discipline yourself to do the same. Some years ago, I came under conviction that I didn't always sing when the congregation sang. My excuse was that I was saving my voice for preaching. Then one day the Holy Spirit said to me (I think the human voice was a minister of music), "What if the people take your preaching no more seriously than you take the singing?" I don't sing very well; but when the congregation sings, I join in with vigor.

> **Some leaders lead by intimidation, some by manipulation, and others by inspiration.**

Participate in Sunday morning Bible study.—Do you attend Sunday morning Bible study? A good use of your time during Sunday morning Bible study is to teach a pastor's class. If you do not teach, attend a class or visit different classes. At first your presence may intimidate the teacher, but they will get used to it and appreciate your presence. Laypersons may not be able to expound Scripture as well as you, but being present in their classes will keep you in touch with their hearts. I still remember illustrations, and especially the tears, of the men's Bible study teacher in the class I attended in my first pastorate.

Participate in the sermon.—Through the years I have discovered that God often speaks more clearly to the preacher through the sermon than to any other person in the congregation. In my third church, I had an unusually gifted group of deacons. Often when I was away, I would ask one of them to fill the pulpit. The very first person to answer the call to preach under my ministry did so as a result of getting under conviction from his own preaching. I pray that you and I may be that sensitive to God' message through the sermons we hear, even if we are doing the preaching.

Grow As a Leader

Paul Powell is absolutely right when he says, "There are at least three leadership styles. There is leadership by *intimidation,* leadership by *manipulation,* and leadership by *inspiration*. Leadership by intimidation is leadership by fear. Leadership by manipulation is leadership by deceit. Leadership by inspiration is leadership by influence. Leadership by influence is ultimately the only way for the pastor of a church to lead."[2]

Don't lead by intimidation.—This method may appear to work for awhile. You may have such a strong personality or you may use your position to frighten people into following you. We all know pastors who have been guilty of strongly implying or even saying, "I know this is the will of God, and if you don't agree with me its because you're not right with God." Some even keep a list of persons who have gotten sick or died. Then the list-keeper declares that these things happened to them because they opposed the pastor's leadership. Don't forget, pastors also answer to God. Sometimes occasions will arise when leaders make strong statements about the will of God, but those occasions will be rare. The occasions must be very serious, and we must know beyond a doubt that we know the will of God. When a leader, without any discussion or allowance for anyone else's understanding of the will of God, constantly declares that he has the last word and that what he says is the will of God, followers begin to get suspicious, and rightly so.

If intimidation is a leadership lifestyle, it is wrong; and in most cases it will not work for long. The leader's credibility will erode; the people will be less and less afraid; and they will turn on the leader with a vengeance. Often those who turn on their leader the strongest will be those who earlier followed him with the strongest devotion. They feel so deceived. At that point, it will not matter what the leader says or does; the people will not believe him.

In some situations, a leadership style of intimidation may work for awhile. If the leader is strong enough, if the supply of people is unlimited, if a strong core of committed followers can be maintained, intimidation brings a lot of what seem like effective results. However, there will be a lot of people hurt along the way. The intimidator is not a servant-leader and is not practicing the lordship of Christ in his own life. When Jesus ceases to be Lord in any leader's life, the leader will self-destruct. An even bigger problem with this leadership style is not practical but theological. It simply does not measure up to the model of kingdom leadership seen in Jesus Christ.

Don't lead by manipulation.—Usually a person can lead a little longer by manipulation than by intimidation. Manipulation is illustrated by the pastor who is always scheming. He cannot allow any committee to function without dealing with members of that committee (one-on-one) to convince them to come to the conclusion he wants. His focus is not on the issues involved. He asks members to influence the committee in a certain direction as a favor to him. He may even imply that it will be beneficial for the committee member to influence others in a certain direction. This style of leadership inevitably expands until the pastor or other leader wants to name every committee member and control every decision (usually through others).

Manipulation is not a matter of the leader speaking up in meeting; others do the speaking for him (he has slyly worked behind the scenes). His motive is not advancement of the kingdom, but, more than anything else, it is self-preservation, self-exaltation, more power, or more money. If a decision does not turn out right, this kind of leader can say that it wasn't his idea or doing. Technically he's right. He didn't speak up in the meeting; he didn't force the decision; others did the work for him. Seldom does this style of leadership produce a big explosion in the church. This kind of leader often can stay indefinitely. However, manipulative leadership usually will be characterized by a gradual decline in attendance. Some will be hurt because they were used by the manipulator. They pushed a particular idea the leader wanted. When it didn't turn out well, they got blamed. They feel betrayed, and rightly so. Others will become frustrated when decisions are made with which they do not agree; but because of the leader's manipulative control, they have no way to give real input. The people's respect and trust for such a leader erodes, but if he is good at manipulation, he can hang on while the congregation gets smaller and smaller. Such a leadership style may be good church politics, but it ought to be beneath the dignity of a God-called kingdom leader.

Lead by inspiration.—Influential, inspirational leadership means leading with integrity. This kind of leadership comes the old fashion way: You earn it. God appoints and the congregation affirms

the true kingdom leader. You do not want to be in any position unless you are sure that God led you there. Even if you feel strongly
led to a particular church, if the congregation does not affirm that
call, you assume that either you or they were wrong. When that
happens, you stay where you are or seek another place of service.

When a pastor leads by influence, he may do some of the same
things the intimidator or manipulator does, but his motive and attitude will be different. A person who leads by influence may suggest individuals to be put on particular committees, but he does
this because of insights and information he has. For example, the
pastor may know that a particular member has expertise in a given
area, that this person is growing in his faith and needs a place of
service, or that a particular person will give needed balance to a
committee. The pastor who leads by influence may meet with the
committee chairperson before the committee meeting; but the pastor's motive is to guide the committee in making sound decisions,
not to manipulate it. The pastor may have background information,
research, and insights that should be shared with the chairperson
and likely the whole committee. If the work of a particular committee is extremely significant, the pastor will likely want to be involved in the entire committee process (he should be ex-officio of
all committees). His participation should be in an open, sincere,
give-and-take manner. He should share what he believes is the will
of God but with the understanding that God may be speaking to
others as well. God uses this process of wise, Spirit-led persons
sharing and seeking the will of God together to sharpen and focus
decisions that, indeed, prove to be the will of God for the congregation.

The kingdom leader must be a good listener. The leader should
listen even when suggestions appear to be absurd. If 99 percent of
the suggestion is foolishness but one percent can be used, it is
worth listening to. Even if 100 percent of the suggestion is useless,
when the person has been heard and affirmed, he or she is more
likely to support the decision that ultimately is made, and you
have maintained fellowship with that person, which is of major
importance.

Learn to say, "I'm sorry." This does not mean that you run
around ringing your hands saying it all the time. But remember,

the only people who don't make mistakes are those who don't do anything. You are going to make mistakes. Even when you are right, sometimes you will make mistakes about how you handled the situation. You will push too hard or not hard enough. You will act too quickly or too slowly. Confess your mistakes. Don't overdo it, but practice saying, "I was wrong." Often your confession can be made to the individual. Sometimes it should be done publicly.

Inspirational leadership inevitably will attract a positive followship.

You'll be amazed that an occasional sincere confession often will gain far more than being right all the time. The truth is, even if we pretend, none us of us are right all the time.

Learn to laugh at yourself. When you mess up, and it's obvious to you and to the people, don't miss a good opportunity to laugh. If you mispronounce a word, say, "Well, I never did learn to say that word," or, "Come on congregation let's say it together." If you announce the Scripture as Joshua 1:1 and you accidentally begin to read from Judges 1:1, say, "Now let's turn to that other Book of Joshua" (then read the correct Scripture), or say, "I always did have trouble finding Joshua. Now let's try that again." Take the ministry very seriously, but do not take the pastor—yourself—too seriously.

If a committee decision caused a problem, don't point your finger at the committee and say, "It's their fault! I didn't have anything to do with it." The pronoun *we* is extremely important. Say, "That didn't go as well as we thought it would, did it? We thought it would work. Now let's trust God to give us a better plan. Remember folks, we're all in this together. God is teaching us and leading us to exactly what He has in mind." Over time, people will learn to trust you and to follow you. When you make mistakes, you'll discover that the people will, in the long run, treat you like you treat them. Life tends to be an echo of our words and actions. Matthew 7:1–5 declares, "Judge not, that ye be not judged. For with what judgment ye judge, ye shall be judged: and with what measure ye mete, it shall be measured to you again. And why beholdest thou the mote that is in thy brother's eye, but considerest not the beam that is in thine own eye? Or how wilt thou say to thy brother, Let me pull out the mote out of thine eye; and, behold, a beam is in thine own eye? Thou hypocrite, first cast out the beam out of thine own eye; and then shalt thou see clearly to cast out the mote out of thy brother's eye."

Inspirational leadership inevitably will attract a positive followship. "Organization doesn't really accomplish anything. Plans don't accomplish anything, either. Theories of management don't much matter. Endeavors succeed or fail because of the people involved. Only by attracting the best people will you accomplish great deeds."3

The inspirational, influential kingdom leader will draw around him the best people—people who love the Lord and follow a kingdom leader. The kingdom leader has a tremendous advantage over any other leader—the promised power of the Holy Spirit. The patient, focused leader under the lordship of Christ is only an instrument of that ultimate influence—the influence and power of God. Therefore, you do not need to intimidate or manipulate. Be who you are: God's man, loving Him and serving with the people He has given you.

Make Changes Correctly

All churches need change, and kingdom leaders are agents of change. Ultimately we cannot change anyone or anything, but Jesus is the miracle worker of change. To be born again is a life-changing experience Once we are born again, spiritual growth brings changes. Growth (change) often is not as rapid as it should be, and it certainly does not follow a straight line of upward progress toward maturity. Indeed, Christian growth, as far as our earthly life is concerned, is never a point of arrival. It is a process, a journey.

A church is a group of born-again believers who covenant together to function as the body of Christ in carrying out our assigned purpose. Thus, the church is made up of believers on a journey. The church, likewise, is a work in progress. Our assignment as kingdom leaders includes enhancing that progress. The church you serve needs change: systems, programs, and people need change. You will not see every needed change occur, but your goal ought to be to leave the church better than you found it.

We work in partnership with the Holy Spirit; we also work with our predecessors and our successors. Your role may be that of building on an idea or dream of your predecessor. Your work may be to prepare the way for the ministry of your successor. Paul said, "I have planted, Apollos watered; but God gave the increase" (1 Cor. 3:6). This principle applies to winning individuals to Christ. It also applies to buildings, programs, procedures, and attitudes.

For example, in all five of my pastorates, my predecessor led the church to build a new building or do extensive remodeling. Each one of them left a debt to be paid. The first two became debt free during my tenure as pastor. The next two became debt free, entered large building programs, and became debt free again. My fifth church built a much needed but expensive building under my predecessor's leadership from which I inherited a huge debt. My pastoral role was to reduce the debt and to put in motion a plan by which the church could rapidly pay off the debt. In each of these examples, my ministry benefited from and was a part of the dream of my predecessor. My fourth pastorate experienced the most rapid growth of any of my churches. I followed a pastor whose ministry did not show numerical growth. Yet, during his years, decisions were made, procedures were established, and positive attitudes were developed. He personally sacrificed to prepare the way for the growth that occurred during my pastorate. Statistically, the rapid growth occurred while I was pastor; but from God's viewpoint, my predecessor received equal credit. Most of us who have been long-term pastors can cite example after example when we have prepared the way for others' ministries or received the benefit from the ministry of others.

Change is not easy, but necessary. Someone has said, "Nobody likes changes except babies, and they cry about it." Every kingdom leader's prayer should be: "God grant me the serenity to accept the things I cannot change, the courage to change the things I can, and the wisdom to know the difference." Wouldn't it be grand if we had a magic formula for change, if everything that needed to be changed could be, and everybody would be happy about it? Wouldn't it be wonderful if every story of change had a happy ending. I've got good news, and I've got bad news. The good news is, there is a way to plan change. The bad news is, the plan doesn't always work.

However, a plan for change is extremely helpful. Let me recommend one. The plan that I share is not original with me, but I do not know where I first came across it. Through the years I have used it, shaped it, and reworded it. I share it with you in the hope that it will help you as it has helped me.

Recognize the need for change.—Every church needs change, but before you set about changing things, ask, What needs to be changed? Is the need for these changes generally recognized by the entire church? Is the need recognized by only a few? Or, do the people see any need for these changes? Ask, What is the history of attempts in the past to make changes in these or similar areas? Are the changes you want to make needed for the sake of the congregation and its purpose, or do you simply want changes that you prefer? Are the perceived changes needed to minister to the current membership and to reach a changing community, or do you want to make these changes to enhance your own ministry image? More importantly, are these changes that God wants made or simply good things you would like to see done? These are questions that you need to ask as you begin to look toward possible change.

Resistance to change frequently depends on the age and personality of the church and persons within the church, especially the power structure.

Likely these things already would have been changed if resistance had not been met. Strong resistance usually is present when change means spending a great deal of money, breaking with long-standing or emotionally-charged tradition, disrupting the comfort level of the people, challenging the authority of the power structure in the church, changing a significant doctrinal position, or adjusting a method of doing missions and ministry.

The degree of resistance to change often is unpredictable. Frequently, resistance depends on the age and personality of the church and persons within the church, especially the power structure. More than anything else, resistance or lack of it is dependent on the relationship between the pastor and the congregation and particularly between the pastor and dominant personalities in the church.

Seeing the need for change may come from the pastor's personal observations or from listening to the people. Most likely, realizing the need for change will come from a combination of the two. God speaks through Bible study, prayer, and the presence of the Holy Spirit. He also speaks through circumstances and the words of others. The real difficulty usually is not in knowing what needs to be changed, but in knowing what needs to be done next.

Educate the congregation about the need for change.—This will include the "why," "what," and possibly "how." "When" usually is not known this early in the process, but will become a key element. Timing is not everything, but it is extremely important. How long do you need to wait before you begin to make changes? Many factors need to be looked at. How threatening is the change? How entrenched is the tradition that will be affected? How widely recognized is the need for change? What is the trust level between the pastor and the people? Do the people understand the change and the need for it, and how willing are the people to support the change?

Generally no big changes need to be made for the first 12 to 18 months of a new ministry. This gives time for a strong trust level to be established. Time spent preaching the Word of God, loving the people, and consistently living out the fruit of the Spirit is never time wasted.

In the analogy of the shepherd and the sheep that is so prominent in the New Testament, Jesus is the Great Shepherd and we are undershepherds (1 Pet. 5:1–4; John 21:15–17). Jesus said of the sheep, "A stranger will they not follow, but will flee from him: for they know not the voice of strangers" (John 10:5). It takes time for the sheep to learn that the undershepherd is not a hireling, that he truly loves the sheep and will lead them faithfully. Simply put, it takes time for the church to learn to trust its leader. It also takes time for the pastor-leader to earn the church's trust and its willingness to follow him. How long this process takes varies. If the church has been misled in the past, gaining its trust may take longer. If the congregation is unusually loyal to a past leader, earning the church's trust may take longer. If the church is in trouble and knows it, the congregation may come quickly to trust its new leader. If an immediate meshing of your and the church's personalities occurs, gaining the church's trust and willingness to follow your leadership may not take long at all. If an error in timing is likely to be committed, usually it is better to move too slowly than too quickly. On the other hand, God did not bring you into leadership to do nothing. So keep the need for change in prayerful focus as you look toward His revealed time.

Taking the time to properly educate the congregation about the need for change is time well spent. This effort may be the most important part of the change process. How do you educate the congregation about the need for change? Talk about the need from the pulpit, in the church newsletter, in meetings, from house to house, everywhere. You need not always initiate the conversation about change and certainly do not need to do all the talking. Listen to the people. They may be further along than you think. You likely will pick up some excellent ideas from them. You may discover resistance that you were not aware of, but you may also discover ways around resistance by listening. Above all, you are establishing relationships of trust.

My friend, who has been successful in business, education, and the church, often says, "I say it and say it and say it until they begin to say it back to me." When they do begin to say it back to you, don't say, "That's what I've been telling you all along!" Instead, affirm the idea as if it originated with them. Then reinforce what they have said.

Another good educational method for the people and for you is the survey. Periodically, give the entire congregation an opportunity for input. The survey can be conducted by a committee, the staff, or the pastor. Use it with integrity. Tell the people what it's for, and use it accordingly. If the survey is for your own information, you do not need to share the information you gain with the congregation. Don't use the survey as a hammer to beat the congregation over the head. Neither is the survey a way of finding out where the congregation is going so that you can get out front and look like a great leader.

A survey is a tool. For example, if you are considering constructing a new building, ask the congregation to fill out a survey form on which you ask 20 or so questions about your current building and the possibility of new buildings. Ask, "Do we need a new sanctuary? Would we be better off to go to two or three worship services? Do we need to build educational space now and a worship center later? If we build a new worship center or an education building, should we wait until we have one-half of the money on hand?" Give the people the opportunity to answer "yes," "no," or "unsure."

Surveys can be taken on a variety of important issues, such as changing worship styles, the time of services, the number of Sunday School or worship times, the method of election or ministry functions of deacons, how new members are received or other constitution and by-law changes, as well as large financial decisions.

No congregation will advance beyond its pastor's leadership.

From a survey, you can learn whether the congregation is ready to vote, whether more education is needed, or whether to drop the matter all together. You are better off for a survey to show a 55–45 split in the congregation over a matter than to have brought it to a vote which revealed a 55–45 split. A survey is not as emotional, as public, or as official and permanent as a vote. Taking a survey heightens the congregation's awareness that a particular is being considered and being prayed over by the church's leadership.

You can hardly overestimate the significance of moving at a reasonable speed (God's speed) and properly educating the congregation on a matter. Henry Blackaby gives us words of wisdom on this matter: "Not only does a church need to know *what* God wants them to do, but they need to know *when* He wants them to do it. We must wait until God's time. . . . The churches I have served have had many traditions. I kept teaching and teaching and teaching until the Spirit of God, who is our common Teacher, brought us to one heart and one mind. . . . I felt that my responsibility as a pastor was to lead God's people into such a relationship with Jesus Christ that they would know clearly when He was speaking. Then I asked them to obey God—not follow a program, an influential lay leader, a committee, or me. God the Holy Spirit is the Christian's real Motivator."[4]

Design progressive steps of action.—Now is the time to use the administrative process. A committee may need to be appointed to

66

develop appropriate steps to make the change, meet the need, or solve the problem. These steps need to be developed, looking at various possibilities. The result of previous surveys may be helpful, or a new one may need to be taken.

How you proceed from here depends on the matter being considered. For example, if the church apparently is ready to proceed with a building program, surveys may educate and focus the congregation on money matters, size and type of building, and timetable for construction. Also, many discussion meetings need to be held. Usually the more the people are involved, the more emotional, monetary, and spiritual support can be expected.

Along the way, the pastor needs to share his heart and vision from the pulpit with the people. Preaching is the most effective way that God has given for His message to be communicated to His church. No congregation will advance beyond its pastor's leadership. The pastor's convictions and leadership are seen clearest in his preaching. The sheep need desperately to see the direction God has given to His appointed shepherd. They need to hear his voice and be assured of God's leadership through him. Preaching encourages and guides.

At what rate should steps toward action be taken? This varies greatly. If the issue is an emotionally-charged matter such as how to elect deacons or define their ministry function, the more the action is discussed the more volatile it can become. On a matter like this, go slowly and be thorough in educating the people. Include surveys and committee discussions, especially with the deacons themselves, but when the Holy Spirit indicates the time is right, move decisively. Frequently, rehashing the same old matters over and over gives the devil the opportunity to divide the church. Sometimes going over and over the same ground can be a delaying tactic used by those who are against the action. Pray for spiritual discernment in knowing when to move forward.

If the matter is clear-cut, such as the meeting times for worship and Sunday morning Bible study, basic questions such as when and how need to be dealt with, but these issues should not require lengthy planning. Make a clear recommendation that anticipates questions and gives reasonable answers. Present a clearly defined, step-by-step timetable, and then move forward. Do thorough study, but do not fall into the trap of studying the issue on and on, ad infinitum. When the planning is complete and God lets you know the timing is right, move to the next step.

Bring the matter to the point of decision by the church.—Use every appropriate means to gather positive support. Other committees or groups besides the recommending committee may be affected by the action. Therefore, discuss the matter with them before asking for church action. Often these committees and groups will affirm their support. If not, it is still better for opposition to be known and the matter discussed in committee rather than on the floor of the church. In many churches, the endorsement of the Church Council is important. In others, affirmation from the deacon body is helpful. The approval of the deacons in every matter considered by the church is not necessary, but affirmation of the deacons as "men of honest report, full of the Holy Ghost and wisdom" (Acts 6:3) is helpful in matters of great significance to a church. Gather appropriate support; bring the matter to the church; and ask for a positive vote.

Giving the church multiple choices in decisions usually is not a good idea. Many choices may divide the church. For example, if you are dealing with a building program, do not ask the church to vote between building nothing at all, building a worship center, or building an educational building; or to vote for doing nothing, building a new building, or remodeling the existing building. The likelihood is that no choice will get a majority vote, the congregation will become divided, and the decision, if any, will be confused.

The recommendation should ask for a clear yes or no vote. Give clear notice of the business meeting and the matter(s) to be considered. Follow the by-laws precisely. Do more than is required. Let the congregation discuss the matter thoroughly. Guide the recommending committee toward a positive presentation. The committee, and certainly the pastor, should not get defensive. Answer questions openly and lovingly. Bring the matter to a vote. Whatever the outcome, believe for this time, God's will has been done. If the recommendation is supported against opposition, don't gloat. If it is voted down, don't pout. As a man of God, speak positively and encouragingly to the congregation, not so much for the action taken but for the spirit of the congregation. Whatever the action, remind the people (and yourself) that the church is God's church, and He is building His kingdom.

Be prepared for accommodations and compromise.—In the process of change, some matters are essential and some are not. If, in a committee meeting or even on the floor of the church, an amendment is made that will facilitate matters and bring more people on board without compromising the intent of the original motion, accept it in good faith. For example, the congregation is dealing with the emotional matter of moving to a deacon rotating system. Feelings are running high, and a motion to amend the original motion is made to allow deacons over age 65 to exempt themselves from the proposed rotating system and be designated deacons emeritus. This accommodation will not hurt the move to a rotating system and will affirm those who have served long and well under the previous system. Let's say that the recommending committee gladly accepts the amendment. The rotating system passes; a deadlock is avoided; and the spirit of the church is enhanced.

While pastor of Central Baptist Church in Corbin, Kentucky, the processes advocated here had been followed all the way down to the recommendation being made to the congregation that the church build a building that would provide education and family-life-center space. Actually, the church needed to build worship space, too, but the congregation had taken prior action to establish multiple services, which supplied worship space. When the recommendation to build was presented, an amendment was made requiring that the church have half of the money on hand for the building before ground breaking occurred. Similar thoughts had been discussed and generally had been accepted anyway. So the pastor spoke in favor of the amendment. When the amendment passed, this accommodation brought on board some who were in opposition because of money concerns. Then a very influential gentlemen with a significant following spoke against the motion, stating that what the church needed was worship space. At this point, the pastor stood and responded by agreeing that worship space was needed, but that educational space was needed first; and that if patience were exercised, enough growth would occur through Sunday School that worship space would be built later, and the church would have both. This simple statement recognized the validity of the opposition and indicated that the need for more worship space would be met. This accommodation lead to an almost unanimous vote of the church to build as recommended. At the close of the business session, the man who had spoken against the building because he wanted worship space, rose to announce his gift of the first $1,000 toward the new building. All decisions do not have that kind of happy ending, but many can if we are willing to allow minor adjustments and deal openly and fairly with opposition.

Focus on issues, not on personalities.

Work for stabilization and reconciliation.— Everybody is not always happy with every decision the church makes. Often when changes are made, good people get their feelings hurt. Most of the time, they are committed Christians who love their church and their Lord. The situation simply is one of good people on both sides of an issue sincerely disagreeing with one another.

Many times making a controversial decision has the effect of rejecting the power and authority of past leaders. Many, many times they are among the most godly people in the church. They may have come into power at a time when somebody needed desperately to step forward and assume leadership. To their credit, they did. The church would not have faired well if they had not. Now, as a result of a decision, new leaders may be stepping forward. This may involve a new leadership style. Past leaders feel rejected, replaced, and left-out.

Once a decision has been made, how do you help those who have been hurt? Do not try to explain away or lessen the significance of the church's decision, but affirm the sincerity and the significance of the persons who may have opposed the decision. Respect and love shown in words, deeds, and attitude are very important. This does not mean that you pamper spiritual babies; it means that you put yourself in their shoes. If you had their perspective, you likely would feel as they feel. Understanding goes a long way.

You may be able to involve the opposition in the carrying out the action in a way that acknowledges their significance and wisdom without compromising the decision. Perhaps they can be affirmed as a vital part of the church in other ways. Such action can be as simple as calling on someone who opposed the action to lead in prayer. At other times a smile, a handshake, or a hug may go a long way. On other occasions, time may be required to heal the hurt of the one who feels offend. Reach out to them when you can. Before you know it, healing has occurred and fellowship has been restored. God has His own way of healing hurts, often to our surprise, but always to His glory.

At the very heart of the whole matter of making changes is that we focus on issues, not on personalities. Simply because someone disagrees with you does not mean they don't like you. To disagree with one another's ideas does not mean that one is smarter, wiser, or more holy than another. Stability and reconciliation grow out of recognition that we are brothers and sister in Christ and that all are essential parts of the body.

Pay Attention to Details

Good leaders delegate and empower others, but they pay attention to details. Very few positive things will happen if they are allowed to drift. Be innovative; do things better than they've ever been done before. Having a good idea, loving the people, sharing the dreams and visions God has given you are not enough. You must plan for today, tomorrow, and 10 years from now. When you go before the Church Council, leadership team, deacons, or a committee, do not simply throw out a problem and ask, "What do you think we ought to do?" It's much better to say, "Here's the problem and a suggested solution. What do you think?"

Allow for maximum participation, but guide the process. You are not a church dictator. You are the church's leader. The church expects you to lead. If you do not lead, someone else will assume the role of leader. The church will lose respect for your leadership, and you may not accomplish what you felt God was leading you and the church to do. Paul did not hesitate to give leadership to the churches. As he wrote about doctrinal error in the Corinthian church, he said, "And the rest will I set in order when I come" (1 Cor. 11:34).

Summary

The Holy Spirit guides churches through persons, particularly through God-called pastors. The Spirit is our Leader, but we are the instruments though whom He leads. That should not surprise us, since "the Word was made flesh, and dwelt among us" (John 1:14).

Jesus, the model kingdom leader, entrusted His mission of redemption to a group of very imperfect disciples and eventually to us. Just as the Spirit and Jesus entrust persons with God's kingdom work and empower them to do it, every kingdom leader must do likewise.

Just as Jesus practiced what He preached, kingdom leaders must live out what they preach, teach, and encourage their churches to do.

More than anyone else, Jesus recognized the need for change and growth in His disciples, but He patiently nurtured them along. He picked them up when they failed and forgave them when they sinned. We also may be the first to recognize the need for change and growth. We may chaff under what we feel are the restrictions of tradition and an unwillingness of the church to move as rapidly as we want. But as Jesus' servant-leaders, we are to follow His example in loving and caring for our congregations. As much as we wish for change, we must not destroy the very church we are attempting to build when we seek to bring about change.

---

[1] Colin Powell, "My American Journey," *American Management Association,* December 1996.
[2] Paul Powell, *Basic Bible Sermons on Handling Conflict* (Nashville: Broadman Press, 1992), 40.
[3] Colin Powell, "My American Journey."
[4] Henry T. Blackaby and Claude V. King, *Experiencing God: Knowing and Doing the Will of God* (Nashville: LifeWay Press, 1991), 169–70.

CHAPTER 5

Church Growth:
Key to a Long and Fruitful Ministry

• •

"He that goeth forth… shall doubtless come again with rejoicing, bringing his sheaves with him"

(Ps. 126:6).

If no growth of any kind—numerical, spiritual, ministry, or missions growth—is occurring in a church, very likely the pastor and the church will grow discouraged, and the pastor's ministry will come to an untimely end. That does not need to happen. All churches can grow in at least one of these areas. Churches that carry out the Great Commission will grow in one or more of these areas. Churches that are not carrying out the Great Commission are not functioning as New Testament churches.

Psalm 126, a great "Song of Degrees" sung by Jewish pilgrims en route to Jerusalem for great feast days, ends with a plea to bring people to God. For the Jews, this meant gathering their people to Israel and to Jerusalem. For us, it means bringing people to Christ for salvation. This emphasis can be seen best in the Great Commission. The Great Commission clearly describes the church's purpose as reaching, baptizing, and teaching people the Word of God. Individual churches should develop their own vision statement and purpose statement from the Commission.

Evangelism is the driving force behind all church growth.

A healthy church that is functioning according to God's will grows, either numerically, spiritually, or both, and will experience ministries expansion and missions advance.[1] Complete kingdom growth is growth in all four areas. Evangelism—doing what the Great Commission commands—is the driving force behind all church growth. Evangelism produces church growth by bringing men, women, boys, and girls to a saving knowledge of Jesus Christ.

Christ's call to every unsaved persons is "Come." He is standing with outstretched arms, pleading, "Come unto me, all ye that labor and are heavy laden, and I will give you rest" (Matt. 11:28). Christ's commission to every Christian is to go make disciples: "Go ye therefore and teach all nations." This call and this commission are basic to biblical evangelism.

Psalm 126:6 declares that if we go forth and weep, we will come again, bringing our sheaves with us: Evangelism will occur. However, evangelism can never be taken for granted or left to chance. For evangelism to occur, we must . . .

Expect a Harvest

One of the key words in Psalm 126:6 is *doubtless*. The word means "no doubt about it." When God's people meet His conditions He gives victory. Jesus came "to seek and to save that which was lost" (Luke 19:10). And, every true kingdom leader will focus on winning souls. When that happens, souls will be saved, Christians will grow spiritually, the church will be strengthened, and the kingdom of God will increase. How many souls will be saved? We do not know! That is not our business; that's God's business. Our responsibility is to sow the seed (the Word of God), to cultivate, and to believe that God will give the increase.

I could refer you to many contemporary examples of evangelistic churches, but my recommendation is that anyone interested in evangelism begin with a study of God's Word. The Bible embodies the principles for growing a church. The Word is the original church growth manual.

From its inception, the New Testament church was a going and sowing church. God honored the church's work with rejoicing because of the precious sheaves (souls) that were gathered. The Book of Acts is filled with phrases such as "the Lord added to the church daily" (2:47), "the number of the disciples was multiplied" (6:1), "a great company of the priests were obedient to the faith" (6:7), and "a great number believed" (11:21). "Added," "multiplied," "great numbers"—these words describe the life of the early church and should characterize the life of our churches today.

A careful study of the spectacular growth of the church in Acts reveals the key principles of church growth that are still applicable.

Make a commitment to share Christ with the unsaved (Acts 1:8).—The pastor must be a consistent winner of souls. *First,* for example's sake. The pastor can hardly get others to win souls if he does not practice soul-winning himself. *Second,* for his own spiritual growth. Winning the unsaved to Christ keeps the pastor's soul on fire with the gospel and his prayer life alive. *Third,* because God expects him to win souls. The devil will do anything in his power to prevent a pastor from going after the lost. A pastor is a busy man. If he does not set aside a definite time for evangelistic visitation, the week will slip by without his having attempted to win anyone to Jesus.

Be committed to constant, fervent prayer (Acts 1:14).—The kingdom leader must be empowered by prayer. The early disciples bathed all that they did in prayer. Prayer gives the church its warmth and fervent spirit. Prayer connects the church to the power of God. Look for ways to call the church to prayer for the salvation of the lost.

Choose effective leaders (Acts 1:24–25).—No organization or institution, including the church, ever rises above its leaders. This includes the pastor, staff, and lay leaders. Seek out persons who are soul-winners to serve as deacons, on committees, and as teachers.

Constantly train soul-winners.—Use your Discipleship Training time to prepare leaders to be soul-winners. Train Sunday School workers in evangelism. Teach them to use the plan of salvation printed in their quarterlies. Show them how to give an invitation in the class. Good leaders well-chosen and well-trained can multiply the pastor's soul-winning leadership.

The church that enlarges its organization promotes growth; the church that does not enlarge its organization stifles growth.

Keep the Bible central (Acts 8:4).—In churches where the greatest growth is occurring, the truth and authority of Scripture are unquestioned. The Bible is preached from the pulpit, taught in the classroom, believed in the pews, and lived on the streets.

Maintain a happy, loving fellowship (Acts 2:46–47).—Churches will grow if a spirit of love, joy, and unity prevails. Soul-winning brings joy. "He that goeth forth and weepeth, bearing precious seed, shall doubtless come again with rejoicing" (Ps. 126:6).

Enlarge the organization (Acts 6:3).—The early church enlarged the organization to meet needs. The "enlargement" principle is a matter of simple multiplication: The larger the organization, the more people you have serving. The more people you have serving, the greater your outreach potential. The greater your outreach potential, the greater your growth. The church that enlarges its organization promotes growth; the church that does not enlarge its organization stifles growth. Enlargement probably will mean new classes, new ministries, more space, and additional staff.

Involve all the people (Acts 8:4).—The pastor's role as kingdom leader is not just to proclaim God's Word. His role also is to equip church members for God's service in teaching, preaching, training, and by example. The more people who are involved, the more effective a church's ministry becomes.

Work hard (Acts 20:31).—Churches need to declare war on laziness. The joy of victory cannot be had apart from personal sacrifice. "He that goeth forth and weepeth, bearing precious seed" describes hard work. But the harvest brings rejoicing.

Reap the Harvest

The harvest involves sowing, cultivation, watering, and reaping. If these essentials are to be done, the field must be located. The truth is, most Christians can count on one hand the number of lost people they personally know. Where do we find prospects?

Register worship service guests.—This is the most obvious place to begin. Those who attend our worship services have shown an interest in our church and their spiritual needs. Develop a system of registering worship service guests that works in your community. Some churches find that it still works to ask guests to remain seated while members and regular attenders are asked to stand. Welcome the guests, share a visitor's information card with them, and ask them to fill it out and place it in the offering plate during the offertory. Often, this is a good time to sing a fellowship hymn or chorus and to encourage the people to greet one another. Most regular attenders like this. It keeps guests from feeling quite as conspicuous as if they were asked to raise their hand or to stand. It also helps worshipers to relax. However, this system of registering guests has two drawbacks: (1) you may have people who have visited your church several times and do not want to be continuously welcomed as visitors; (2) some people still are intimidated by being identified as a guest, even by sitting while others are standing.

Others churches have found that a better way is to ask everyone present to register. A list is passed down each pew, and everyone records his or her name and address. This procedure will alert you to persons who have been attending for some time and have stopped filling out visitor's cards. An even better way is to have a visitor-information tear-off tab on your worship bulletin. Guests can fill out and tear off this tab and drop it in the offering plate without feeling like they are being pointed out. Trained greeters can help identify, welcome, and assist guests at the beginning and close of the worship service.

For many years, the deacons at Central Baptist Church, Winchester, Kentucky, have made brief visits immediately after worship to the home of every visitor. The deacons simply thank the people for attending, answer any questions they might have about the church, and, if possible, gather additional information. This is a vital ministry that deacons can perform in any church.

Take a door-to-door survey.—This still works in most places. Gather a group of people on Sunday afternoon. Train them in the basics of making a good impression and getting information. Keep the questions simple: When you go to church, where do you attend? Do you attend weekly, monthly, seldom? Would such programs as activities for senior adults, single adults, preschoolers, children, youth, or parents be helpful to you and your family? May I please have your name and address so that we can provide you with more information about out church? Keep good records and follow up by mail and appropriate visits.

Take a telephone survey.—Go through the phone book or the appropriate section of larger phone books number by number. Ask the same questions that have been suggested for the door-to-door survey. Follow up the calls in the same way you followed up the home calls.

Add to the survey information by periodically visiting the courthouse or utilities agencies and making a list of new homeowners (this information is a matter of public record). Cross reference the names you get from these sources with names in the phone book. This will identify most in-town movers. Write each of the newcomers a welcome letter. Include information about your church. Often a volunteer, or more than one if the town is large and growing, can be enlisted to visit all newcomers. Frequently greeting programs such as Welcome Wagon will include your material and supply you with information about newcomers for a fee. Be aware, however, that much of this information can be somewhat dated when you get it.

Publicize your church.—As you study your community, learn what media outlets are the most effective in communicating with people. In some areas, cable TV access is readily available. In my two most recent pastorates, services were broadcast on local cable free. One of the factors in the rapid growth at Central Baptist Church, Corbin, Kentucky, was our being the first congregation to use television effectively. The pastor's auditorium class and evening worship services were shown live. The second morning worship was rebroadcast the following Sunday morning at 8:30 a.m. That seems to be the ideal time for preaching to non-churchgoers as well as to those who are getting ready for church.

Radio broadcasts can be effective. The most effective broadcasts during my ministry were at Southside Baptist Church, Princeton, Kentucky. I used six one-minute broadcasts that contained Scripture, a devotional thought, and the identification of the pastor and church. These broadcasts were floating time slots between songs played on the secular radio station. What a wonderful way to speak to people who otherwise would not have heard even a verse of Scripture in a typical day. Then at Central Baptist Church, Corbin, Kentucky, a five-minute "Word from the Word of God" was very effective at a typical wake-up time for a clock radio, 6:30 a.m. Many people began their day by hearing this short message.

Use the newspaper to advertise your church. In small towns, weekly newspapers can be especially effective. Some simple suggestions: We live in a people-conscious world. The first thing your eyes go to when you turn the page of a newspaper is a picture, usually of a person. So, use the pastor's picture or occasionally the picture of someone else in the congregation along with an invitation to Sunday morning Bible study and worship. Do not clutter the ad. Leave lots of white space. Change the ad every week by including sermon titles. This communicates that what is happening is important because you keep the message up-to-date. Frequently change the format of the ad.

Take advantage of special events such as revivals, musicals, dramas, recognitions, and anniversaries to secure publicity. Write an article on the event. Enclose a picture whenever possible. Most newspaper will run any news-worthy article which you supply them. Their business is to serve the community of which the church is a vital part.

Use Dial-a-Devotion as a ministry and as a means of getting out the gospel. Periodically, I have shared the plan of salvation with callers. Of the 200 to 300 persons who have called daily through the years, I'm sure that many of them were lost.

Use every appropriate means in your community to get out a positive word about your church. God will use it to reach the lost and the unchurched.

Heighten Evangelism Through Planning
The farm imagery in Psalm 126—sowing, cultivating, and reaping—involved planning. Likewise, good planning is imperative for

the evangelistic church. Someone has said, "To fail to plan is to plan to fail." Planning and special events are imperative. Plan an annual evangelism calendar. Keep it simple. Only put on paper what you really intend to do. The following is an example:

January.—On the first Sunday of the new year, preach a sermon that asks every member to commit to focus on five people for whom they will pray and with whom they will seek to share their faith during the new year. Give the congregation the opportunity to make a note of these names. In the sermon, briefly overview how to lead a person to Christ.

February.—Attend the state evangelism conference. Meet with Sunday School workers before and after evening worship on the third Sunday evening to talk about the up-coming high attendance day and revival. On the third Monday night conduct or attend a one-night associational evangelism workshop; especially encourage your members to attend. Conduct an in-church "I know a prospect" survey in Sunday School and the worship service on the fourth Sunday morning.

March.—On the second Sunday, begin a Sunday School enlargement campaign aimed toward a revival beginning the fourth Sunday in April.

April.—Conduct a telephone blitz, inviting people to attend Sunday School and worship on Easter Sunday. Continue Sunday School promotion. Lead special prayer meetings for revival each Wednesday of the month. Enlist persons to pray around the clock the night before the revival. Ask a volunteer to organize the 24 hours of prayer. The pastor and staff will make evangelistic visits every afternoon or evening the week before the revival. Conduct a one-day soul winning seminar the day before the revival begins. Focus on revival attendance promotions.

May.—Conduct revival follow-up on evangelistic prospects. Make sure new members are enrolled in Sunday School and begin "Survival Kit for New Christians" training. Finalize plans for Vacation Bible School.

June.—Conduct Vacation Bible School. Share the gospel with older children. Follow up on unchurched parents found through Vacation Bible School.

July.—Finalize plans for fall revival scheduled for late October.

August.—Do a community house-to-house survey.

September.—Begin an eight-week Sunday School promotion in conjunction with a sister church to climax on revival Sunday. Conduct a youth evangelism training session using WOW witnessing material.

October.—Continue Sunday School promotion. Lead special prayer meetings for the revival each Wednesday of the month. Pastor and staff will make evangelistic visits every afternoon or evening the week before revival. Conduct a one-day soul winning seminar the day before the revival. Focus on revival attendance. Especially promote youth attendance. Use drama and youth music during the revival services, and special on youth night.

Do not leave behind many of your current members in your attempt to reach new people.

November.—Do revival follow-up on evangelistic prospects. Make sure new members are enrolled in Sunday School and begin *Survival Kit for New Christians* training.

December.—Review evangelism plans for the coming year. Touch base with evangelists who have been scheduled for the next three years. Begin to publicize plans for next year's evangelism efforts.

Your evangelism planning can be much more sophisticated than the above suggestions. Certainly, I would encourage you to use a variety of evangelistic activities during the year. My point is to encourage you to plan regularly and early for evangelism. Otherwise, evangelism has a way of falling through the cracks.

Magnify Evangelism Through Worship

This is a day of transition in worship. Many new methods are being used by the church to enhance worship, and many of them are being blessed by the Lord. We used a number of these methods, such as drama, interpretative movement, choruses, and contemporary music, especially involving our youth at Central Baptist Church, Winchester, Kentucky.

Many of us like a sense of freedom and openness in worship, but everyone does not share our likes and dislikes. Therefore, worship leaders should introduce change in worship styles slowly, patiently and with the highest affirmation of traditional worship. Make sure your congregation does not misunderstand what you are doing. Do not leave behind many of your current members in your attempt to reach new people. Focus on the basics. The three core issues in evangelistic worship are:

Talk with God in sincere prayer.—Involve the congregation in prayer. Use the laity to lead in prayer. Pray for real needs. Use whatever methods successfully encourage prayer among the people you lead.

Communicate the message of Christ musically.—As a nonmusician, but a lover of music that honors God and relates to the people, may I make some suggestions to music leaders about a music that encourages evangelism:

Make the prelude music lively and enjoyable. Do not become frustrated if the people get a little noisy visiting with each other while enjoying the music.

Begin the worship service on time with a call to worship or a praise hymn that is up-beat, and keep the service moving with a sense of direction.

Don't be tempted to preach between hymns. Remember, singing is not primarily presentation; it is participation. Congregational singing is the most important music in the worship service. Let them sing!

Sing "heart" music, the kind of music that appeals to the unchurched and new attenders as well as the majority of your congregation. Do not pitch your service toward the few trained musicians in the congregation.

Coordinate the music with the drama (if used) and the sermon. Get the preacher to the pulpit on time; and participate in the sermon, especially if you sit on the platform. Open your Bible and read the sermon text, follow the sermon, and perhaps take notes. You can set an example for the congregation and be a real encourager to the preacher.

Be ready for the invitation. Have the invitation hymn number ready. Move into position and begin the song in coordination with the pastor's lead-in to the invitation. Sing softly and encouragingly. If you change invitational hymns, always move to one the congregation knows by heart. Never sing new hymns for invitations. When people leave the service, they are much more likely to be humming one of the songs from the service than they are to be reciting a point of the sermon. Music communicates, especially today. Use it as an opportunity to tell the wonderful news of the gospel.

Proclaim the gospel through preaching.—Preaching does as much as or more than any other single worship element to create atmosphere. Preaching that comes from a warm, compassionate heart will stir people to action. Years ago, C. E. Matthews said, "Eggs are not hatched in a refrigerator. Neither are Christians inspired to win souls in a spiritually cold atmosphere. The right kind of preaching produces the right kind of atmosphere in a church."[2]

In "Preaching That Endures," I shared my conviction that the best preaching is expository, extemporaneous, and enthusiastic; but more important than form is the spirit in which preaching is done. True evangelistic preaching that God honors comes from the preacher who has spent time with Christ in prayer, sought and found the message for the hour through Spirit-guided Bible study, and has sought to lead someone to a saving relationship with Jesus Christ during the week. Without that preparation, whether the preacher speaks with eloquent voice or a stammering tongue, he will not do evangelistic preaching. The preacher who has been alone with Christ will lift Him up and He will honor His promise that "and I, if I be lifted up from the earth, will draw all men unto me" (John 12:32).

Summary

The kingdom leader is in partnership with the Living God, who promises to bless the faithful, loving, fervent witness with a harvest of souls. "He that goeth forth and weepeth, bearing precious seed, shall doubtless come again with rejoicing, bringing his sheaves with him" (Ps. 126:6).

---

[1] Gene Mims, *Kingdom Principles for Church Growth* (Nashville: Convention Press, 1994), 108.

[2] C. E. Matthews, *Every Christian's Job* (Nashville: Broadman Press, 1951), 4.

CHAPTER 6

Administration: The Nuts and Bolts of Effective Leadership

• •

"He that goeth forth…, bearing precious seed"
(Ps. 126:6).

The psalmist called on God's people to go forth "bearing precious seed." Who is to go, why we are to go, where we are to go, and what we are to do have been determined by the Great Commission and our vision statement. We must determine how we are to go and how we will scatter the seed. In short, we must have a plan and an organizational structure for carrying out the Commission and our vision statement. Without an organizational structure, the church is like a body without a skeleton. Without administration, the church's plans and resources cannot be focused on its purpose.

Every program, every church organization, and every activity must have organization and administration. Organization and administration are like the drive train of an automobile. They apply divine power and human strength to the tasks at hand and determine how the church will respond to Christ's call in the Great Commission.

To begin, let's explore the valid biblical functions of the church.

> Organization and administration are like the drive train of an automobile. They apply divine power and human strength to the tasks at hand.

The Biblical Functions of the Church

Some think the church has seven scriptural functions; some think it has four; and some six. Gene Mims' book *Kingdom Principles for Church Growth* suggests five. Little is gained by debating the number of valid church functions. Much is gained by seeking to perform these functions.

All five functions are vital to a strong, healthy, growing church. As Dr. Mims writes, "These five functions may not be new to you; neither will they seem profound. You may have heard these functions so often they have lost meaning for you. Even so, they produce profound, life-changing effects when they are put into practice.... They must become active, living principles in our lives before we can experience their God-given power in church growth."[1]

A church should emphasize all five functions at the same time. However, a church may place special emphasis on one or more of the functions at any given time. Each church must determine in its own soul what its most urgent needs are and what functions need special attention. The ideal is for all five functions to be performed continually in a healthy fashion; but reality is that from time to time, fine tuning of the church's emphases will be required.

Evangelism.—Evangelism is reaching out to lost people with the gospel with the purpose of leading them to a saving relationship with Jesus Christ. Saying "everything we do is evangelism" is not enough. Evangelism must be intentional; and the truth is, most of what we do is not intentional evangelism. To do evangelism as it should be done, the driving force of every organization, every program, every budget, and special activities must be evangelism.

Discipleship.—Discipleship is the process by which believers

86

grow in an increasingly intimate relationship with Jesus Christ and become increasingly more useful in His service. This process is life-transforming as the Holy Spirit is allowed to take more and more control of believers' lives.

Among the wonderful results of discipleship is an increasing Christian maturity. The church has the responsibility to provide maximum opportunities for individual and churchwide discipleship development. Discipleship is not just the responsibility of the Discipleship Training program. It is the responsibility of the Bible teaching program, the worship services, the mission program, music program, age-group programs, recreation, and every other church organization, program, and activity.

Ministry.—Ministry is reaching out to people and meeting their needs, whether they are inside or outside the church. It is sharing Christ's love with individuals and performing deeds of service that reflect His love. Ministry sees the value of every person because God sees the value of all persons, so great a value, in fact, that He gave His only begotten Son, the Lord Jesus Christ, to die for the sins of the world (John 3:16). Ministry is seeing what God is doing in the world about us and joining Him in that ministry.

Fellowship.—No other fellowship is like Christian fellowship. Christian fellowship grows out of our common experience in Christ, bearing one another's burdens, and social relationships within a Christian context. Fellowship also grows out of Christians sharing in the church's God-given vision. Sharing in that vision and in the process of carrying it out gives us a sense of ownership in the church and God' kingdom. It strengthens and encourages us to live devoted lives as faithful followers of Jesus Christ. Christian fellowship doesn't just happen. It must be cultivated through every available means to be kept warm and vibrant. It should be encouraged in our families, church organizations, and throughout the entire church.

One of the great things about the church in Acts is that it was "in one accord." That kind of oneness must be true of our churches. Otherwise, we will not have the power to evangelize the world; neither will our testimonies ring true to the unsaved. Didn't Jesus say, "By this shall all men know that ye are my disciples, if ye have love one to another" (John 13:35)?

Worship.—Worship is our personal and congregational experiences with God. Through worship we experience His incredible love for us and respond by expressing our sincere love for Him. Certainly, the worship experience is what the worship service is all about, but worship should occur in Bible study classes, Discipleship Training groups, through mission education and involvement, other church activities, and in the devotional life of the individual.

Evaluating Results

When a church is functioning in a balanced, healthy fashion, certain results will occur. If these results are occurring in your church, keep on doing what you're doing. Enhance and improve those areas that could be done better. If your church is not functioning as it should, numerical growth, spiritual growth, expansion of ministries, and missions advance will not be occurring as they should.

Evaluation is an ongoing process.

Here are some questions you can ask as you attempt to evaluate your church: Are we reaching new people with the gospel? Does a spirit of unity prevail in the church? Are individual lives being changed? Are we expanding our ministries to touch a needy world, near at hand and far away? Does our giving and our going show that we have the world on our hearts?

Some results (or lack of them) are harder to measure that others. Counting the number of people in attendance is much easier than measuring the degree of spiritual growth that is occurring in believers' lives. We can evaluate the percentage of our budgets given to missions and the new missions started more easily than we can see ministry needs out there that our spiritual blindness has kept us from seeing.

How do we evaluate our churches' progress toward fulfilling the Great Commission and our vision statement? We hold up our vision statement to constant review. We observe what going on in us, our churches, and the world about us. Then we determine how well we are doing. Gene Mims and Mike Miller have an excellent evaluation process outlined in *Kingdom Principles Growth Strategies.* I highly recommend that you get a copy of this material and follow it carefully.

Evaluation is an ongoing process, but we must not become so involved in evaluation and analysis that we neglect the very purpose for which we have been called.

Decide on a Primary Church Growth Method

No church can give full emphasis to every function and every program at the same time or all of the time. Examining your church in light of its biblical functions will help you see what aspects of your church need special attention. When problems are dealt with and solved, the church will maintain health and balance. When the church is healthy, it will grow. How can you help the church to stay healthy? By dealing with the problems and needs on an organizational basis.

No organization or activity of a church can exempt itself from any of the church's five biblical functions. However, each organizations has a stronger responsibility for certain functions that are the organization's particular assignment.

When we mention worship, we think immediately of the worship services. Discipleship Training carries the major responsibility in the church for discipling believers. Evangelism brings to mind such things as the outreach visitation program, revivals, and preaching. Ministry events often are organized by mission organizations. Fellowship planning may be the primary responsibility of a committee or a program organization, but fellowship, training disciples, evangelism, worship, and ministry are the responsibility of every organization and activity.

When we begin to pray over our vision, our biblical functions, and the expected results, we begin to look for a method, a focus, a system. The question is, where can we find a method for leading the church in the direction God wants it to go? Today, perhaps more than at any time in recent years, various systems for growing church are being advocated. Which one works best? It depends on the church's cultural and social setting, the congregation's views, and especially the leaders' gifts and interests.

My favorite college football team, a Division 1A team in the powerful Southeastern Conference, hired a new coach from a Division 2 school. The coach is a strong advocate of a wide-open pass-oriented offense. His strongest rival in his previous conference has been quite successful using a strong running offense. Their football philosophies and game plans are totally opposite, but both are successful coaches. When the Division 1A coach's rival was asked whether the new coach could be successful using the passing game in a much stronger conference, he said about the coach's game plan: "It works . . . the thing about it is, it's a system. Hal and I talk about this all the time. He likes to throw the ball, and I like to run the ball. But we both have systems that we believe in and we know how to coach. That's the most important thing."[2]

That's the secret. To be successful, a leader must have a vision and a system of operation that he believes in with all his heart. This requires that the kingdom vision be from God and that the system he uses be the one God has given him. Then he and his congregation will be united in the kingdom's work.

> **To be successful, a leader must have a vision and a system of operation that he believes in with all his heart.**

Under God, the leader must be a good coach. Peter put it like this: "The elders who are among you I exhort, I who am a fellow elder and a witness of the sufferings of Christ, and also a partaker of the glory that will be revealed: Shepherd the flock of God which is among you, serving as overseers, not by constraint but willingly, not for dishonest gain but eagerly; nor as being lords over those entrusted to you, but being examples to the flock; and when the Chief Shepherd appears, you will receive the crown of glory that does not fade away" (1 Pet. 5:1–4, NKJV).

What vision and system has God given you? Have you shared them with your people? Have they become their vision and system? Then give them your best. Keep sharing your vision and system with the people. Do the work of a leader, and lovingly guide your people.

Great churches are being built using aggressive, confrontational evangelism. The focus of the congregation, led by the pastor, is one-on-one soul winning. This method may involve extensive use of Continuing Witness Training, Evangelism Explosion, the Four Spiritual Laws, the Roman Road, or a new and exciting resource called F.A.I.T.H., available from the Baptist Sunday School Board. F.A.I.T.H. is the result of marrying the Bible Teaching-Reaching Division's emphasis on outreach with the Pastor-Staff Leadership

Department's emphasis on evangelism. You will want to familiarize yourself immediately with this new witnessing resource.

God may or may not place one of these systems for growing the church and the kingdom on your and your people's hearts. Even so, evangelism must be the number one objective of the church, and God certainly will give you a system for reaching people for Christ and growing your church.

Evangelism is not optional. It is the heart of the Great Commission (Matt. 28:19–20), and should be the central focus of the church's vision statement. Further, every Bible-believing congregation must have a plan for training soul-winners and an on-going outreach visitation program.

Other great churches are growing by focusing primarily on their worship services. This approach may involve traditional services or more contemporary, seeker-sensitive services. In many communities the worship service approach to evangelism is more compatible with the people's age and lifestyle. Persons in these communities seem to respond more readily to worship-centered outreach.

Whether worship-centered evangelism is your primary approach, worship must be a priority in your church. Corporate worship is at the heart of who we are and what we are about as the people of God. Nothing could be more important than opportunities for believers, collectively and individually, to encounter the living God. In worship, we need to express our love to Him and savor His incredible love for us. As important as worship services are, they may not be the primary means that God has given you and your people to reach out to your community.

A third means of evangelism—and there are many others—is an aggressive Bible teaching-reaching program through Sunday School. My experience has led me to believe in Sunday School as a wonderful means of church growth. Whether you use one of the evangelism plans mentioned or some other, be sure it is the plan God wants you to use where you are. Study it thoroughly, and use it intensively.

Use Your Sunday School

Pastors have a tendency to become consumed by their passion to preach and the demands of pastoral ministries. The danger is that they may neglect their strongest resource for ministry and growth—the Sunday School. Today, particularly, small groups are needed for fellowship, ministry, and outreach. In most churches, these groups already are in place in the Sunday School. Frequently, these groups are not functioning anywhere near their potential. If, however, the pastor is willing to learn and apply basic principles of Sunday School work, this organization can become a mighty army for God. Very likely, the leaders in your church already are enrolled in Sunday School. The genius of Sunday School is, not only is it responsible for Bible teaching, it also can mobilize large numbers of persons for kingdom service.

Arthur Flake said: "The Sunday School presents an unparalleled opportunity for the successful promotion of practically every phase of church activity as well as the utilization of every member of the church and congregation in useful service without detracting from the effectiveness of the Sunday School as a Bible teaching agency, or interfering, in the least degree, with the work of any other desirable and useful church agency." [3]

In many of our churches, the Sunday School either needs to be encouraged, revitalized, or both. This can happen through the example of the pastor's leadership. That example is vital! A church may have a gifted vocational minister of education, a committed Sunday School director, or both. Even so, if the Sunday School is to be strong, it needs the enthusiastic support by the pastor from the pulpit as well as his personal leadership.

What are some of the ways a pastor can be involved positively in Sunday School? He can be a catalyst for helping some basic things happen that will give the Sunday School a leadership role in church growth. Some of these things are:

Start new units.—A class that has been in existence for a number of years with a consistent attendance is not likely to grow or to do breakout ministry and outreach. However, it can help start a new class that will grow. Amazingly, by starting a new class, the sponsoring class often will be revitalized. Starting new classes to foster new growth should be done primarily in the adult area. Classes for other ages often will begin in response to growth.

In starting new classes, begin with a vision. Use the principles of Sunday School growth as illustrations and application in your sermons. Conduct training sessions with workers in which you talk about the principles of starting new classes. Ask God to show you the class that is most receptive to beginning a new class. Talk with the teacher and ask for permission to talk with the class about beginning a new class. In the presentation explain that no one who is not willing to leave the current class will be encouraged to leave. After you have made the presentation, give the idea time to grow. Pray that God will give you a teacher from the sponsoring class to lead the new class.

When the time is right, a minimum of four persons (or if the class is to be a couples class, three couples) should be enlisted to accept the vision of beginning a new class. It often helps if the persons who are beginning the new class are from the younger half of the sponsoring class. This seems to make it more appealing for class members to come out to start a new class. Reassure other members of the existing class that they may stay where they are. Compliment the teacher and the existing class for their willingness to begin a new class. Frequently, within weeks the sponsoring class will build its numbers back to where they were. Within 18 months, the new class likely will be as large as the one out of which it came.

Theoretically, as long as workers are being trained, space is being provided, and new units are being started, a Sunday School can double its size every 18 months. Actually, if a smaller Sunday School starts a couple of new units a year, it is doing well. Larger Sunday Schools ought to begin more. New units may be like existing units, or they may be in specialized areas of need such as classes for singles, special education classes, in-depth Bible study classes, new member orientation classes, or other needs-focused classes. They may be new couples classes or separate classes for men and women. A pastor's class (to be discussed later) can be a new way to reach out to new people.

Increase enrollment.—Lead your Sunday School to develop an open enrollment policy. Ask people to enroll at the first opportunity. Do not remove names from the class roll unless the persons die, move away, join another church, or ask you to take them off. Persons may be asked to enroll even before they attend. When I was pastor of Southside Baptist Church, Princeton, Kentucky, we knocked on the doors of large segments of the town every six months for four years and literally invited people to enroll on the spot. I was amazed at how many enrolled and even more amazed at how many actually attended Sunday School. This effort at the very least communicated to the people of the town that we wanted them in our Sunday School, and it created a sensitivity in the Sunday School to making outreach a lifestyle.

Conduct a high attendance day.—The Sunday School gives the church an opportunity to involve people in outreach who never would have the courage to witness for Christ in any other way. We have many effective Sunday School attendance promotion programs. Here is an example that God used like nothing else in my ministry in 54 Sunday School enlargement efforts involving three churches over a period of 27 years. Forty-eight times the churches involved recorded the highest attendance in their history. A church averaging 125 in Sunday School had a high attendance of 187. A church averaging 945 in Sunday School had a high attendance of 1,496. Twenty percent of the increase continued in Sunday School in the weeks that followed high attendance day. For example, if a church that is running 100 in Sunday School has 150 on high attendance day, the average in the weeks to follow will likely be 110.

Make much of reaching a goal. The celebration of victories is very important to the morale of a church. Praise the Lord! Brag on the people! The people will feel good about themselves and their church. The church will get a vision of its every-Sunday potential.

If you miss a high attendance goal, immediately focus on the positives. Was it the most in one year? Ten years? Was it more than the same Sunday a year ago? Was it more than you would have had without the effort? In some authentic way, focus on the best aspects of the effort.

In conducting the high attendance day, planning and preparation are vital. A six weeks sign-up period has worked best in my experience. A by-product of the work and promotion you do will be an attendance increase as you build toward high attendance day. Make you goal realistic and challenging, a little higher than you reached on your last high attendance day. Don't make the goal unreachable. It's better to have 160 when your goal was 150 than to have 160 with a goal of 175.

Ask people to sign a commitment card such as "Unless providentially hindered, I will be in Sunday School at [church name] Baptist

Church, Sunday, [date], at [time]." This commitment card is very important. Most people who sign the card will be present in your Sunday School on high attendance day. The card also gives your people something concrete with which to approach prospective attenders. People who never would go on visitation, make a phone call, or otherwise extend an invitation to people to come to church often will take a card and ask a friend to sign up.

Good visuals always help. You may wish to use a string of fish, hearts, sheep, or similar items to make a visual display of the number who have committed themselves to be present on high attendance day.

With fish, for example, the theme is "Fishers of Men." The fish displays are placed in the auditorium or in a nearby hallway so that they are highly visible to the congregation. Each class or department has a big fish under which are smaller "blank" fish. The big fish has the name of the class or department, the name of the teacher or director, and the class or department goal. (If the class or department sets its own the goal, it is more likely to work harder to reach the goal.) As persons are signed up to attend, the signed fish is attached over the blank fish. The blank fish should be white and the signed fish could be green or blue. You might want to use gold to represent prospects and visitors, indicating they are special.

A key to reaching any goal is motivation. Enthusiasm, especially on the part of the leaders, helps motivate other members. The pastor absolutely must get excited about high attendance goals. His excitement will penetrate classes and departments, who will welcome new people with open arms. Many of the newcomers can be enrolled, and many will come back. During as well as following the campaign, new units often can be started. High attendance becomes part of the process of ongoing church growth.

What I have shared is simple, but it is worth your time and energy. May I give a testimony? I began a pastorate years ago where the attendance had been declining for a number of years. As I reviewed the church records, looking toward the beginning of a revival meeting, I discovered that only on four occasions in the previous decade had the church had more than 500 in Sunday School. Three of those Sundays were Easter, and the fourth was when a remodeled auditorium was dedicated. Three decades before, the church had its highest one-day attendance of 714.

With this information, a Sunday School potluck dinner was held during which I shared a challenge. The workers, members, and pastor decided in that meeting that to shoot for the all-time high attendance was unrealistic, so we set a goal of 600-plus. The theme was "The Most in a Decade." The minister of music developed a song entitled, "Six Hundred One" to the tune of "Love Lifted Me." Enthusiasm began to mount.

On high attendance day, our Sunday School not only reached the goal, but had an all-time high of 770. The celebration of the victory was fantastic. Plans were made to increase our units and to focus on enrolling new people. A vision was caught for having that many in Sunday School every Sunday. We adopted a goal of increasing average attendance by 100 each year with two annual high attendance days at the heart of the effort. In five years, the average attendance was 801 for the year and eventually grew to 945. Two high attendance days a year continued to be at the heart of efforts to reach people for Bible study through Sunday School. This momentum last for 12 years. What did God use to grow our church? Successful high attendance days!

Start a Pastor's Class

Today, people have two almost contradictory desires in their lives—a hunger for spiritual knowledge and a determination to preserve their anonymity. Because of these two factors, one of the most effective instruments in my ministry for growing churches in three different settings over more than 20 years has been the pastor's auditorium class. Indeed, the pastor's auditorium class can be used effectively by many pastors to reach a group of people who are almost unreachable by any other means.

Some words of caution are in order before you begin a pastor's auditorium class. Start by opening lines of communication with the general leadership of the Sunday School and especially with the adult teachers. You will want to meet with them individually or as a group. This is so important because if teachers do not understand the principles of a pastor's auditorium class they often feel threatened by it. Assure your teachers that no one who is a member of their classes will be allowed to attend the pastor's auditorium class.

96

By mutual agreement, you may focus your enlistment efforts on persons they have been unable to reach for their classes.

Strongly emphasize the partnership idea. Growing a church is a team effort. Before you begin the pastor's auditorium class, you also will want to take time—in print and from the pulpit—to emphasize repeatedly what you intend to do. Try to make sure no one misunderstands either your plans or your motives. Explain that the pastor's auditorium class can be a means of bringing in large numbers of people. Many of them eventually can be encouraged to go into other adult classes, and new classes can be started out of the pastor's auditorium class.

How big should a pastor's auditorium class become? That depends on a lot of factors. At Southside Church, the pastor's auditorium class began with five persons and never reached more than 50 over a period of four years, but it made a major contribution to the church's growth by moving person into other classes. At Central Church, Winchester, Kentucky, over a period of three years the highest number in attendance at any one time was about 65. Again, that many or more moved through the pastor's auditorium class into other classes. At Central Baptist in Corbin, Kentucky, the first Sunday we had 50 in the pastor's auditorium class, and it grew over 12 years to more than 200 on a typical Sunday. Probably 250 to 300 passed through the pastor's auditorium class to become regular members of other classes. Four adult classes began with its nucleus, including the teacher, coming from the pastor's auditorium class.

Although the goal is to move people into other classes, some of those who come into the pastor's auditorium class have never attended Sunday School before, and they will stay with the class indefinitely.

A good way to begin a pastor's auditorium class is in connection with a high attendance day. Gather a list of inactive church members, members and nonmembers who attend worship but not Sunday School, and church prospects who have not started to Sunday School. Write notes to these adults inviting them to be present on the first Sunday of the pastor's auditorium class. If you need to give more details about the class, you can use a duplicated longer letter; but the personal touch of a hand-written note is very important.

Include a self-addressed, stamped postcard on which you ask them to check one of four items: "(1) I will be present in the pastor's auditorium class on [date class begins]. (2) I can't be present on [date class begins], but I think the pastor's auditorium class is a good idea. (3) I am not interested in attending the pastor's auditorium class. (4) Comments." Leave space for them to make any comment they wish.

A list of prospects can be gathered from these responses. Others can be found by scanning the telephone directory and by talking with people at sporting events or other public gatherings. You can locate prospects anywhere you meet people. Make phone calls. Enlist volunteers to help. Periodically write notes to attenders and prospects.

If at all possible, do newspaper or radio advertising. If you have an answering machine at church, promote the pastor's auditorium class on it. Call it "The Most Unusual Bible Study in [name of your town]" or some other interesting name. Print an attractive flyer to mail and leave in restaurants, doctor's offices, on doors, and in other places. Communicate that you teach the Bible and that they really are wanted. Assure prospects that they will never be called upon to pray, read, or make comment.

Teach the Bible, using an informal, conversational lecture method. You do not have to spend long hours in preparation. Simply read a paragraph or chapter of the Bible. Then go back and read a verse or two and comment until you have worked through the passage. Much of your teaching will come out of the overflow of previous study. You may want to use the *Exploring the Bible Series* of Sunday Bible study literature, the *Winter Bible Study* material, or some similar planned study. You may want to take a book of the Bible and teach through it. If you do, be sure to choose one of the shorter books that is easily understood. Don't bog down in a long book, and don't get too "weighty." Remember, you are teaching people who are not used to attending Sunday morning Bible study. Carefully explain the details of the Scripture. Make doctrinal applications, and especially relate the teaching to life.

After the pastor's auditorium class is going strong, you will want to remind members as a group and sometimes one-on-one that other types of classes are available for them to attend. Occasionally invite teachers from the other adult classes to come in and get acquainted with the pastor's auditorium class and to invite class members to visit their classes. Don't push that option so hard that you give the impression that you want your class members to leave. Just help them feel free to go to any other class at any time. Remember, new classes can be started out of the pastor's auditorium class, and potential teachers will emerge from the class.

Some things are very important to the success of the pastor's auditorium class:

The class must be in the auditorium.—People who have attended church only few times, if any, are more comfortable in the auditorium than in a classroom room. They feel less threatened by the large open space. Usually, if they have been to church at all they have been in the auditorium. If they know where anything is at the church, they will know were the auditorium is, and it's usually easy to direct someone to the auditorium. Frequently people who only attend worship services will begin to come earlier and earlier. Before long they will be present for the pastor's auditorium class. Because of the class's location, I suggest starting a little later, perhaps 15 minutes later, than other classes. Stop in plenty of time, perhaps 20 minutes before the worship service is to begin, so that the class will not interfere with those coming in for the worship service. This early stopping time also will give the pastor a few minutes to rest and prepare for the worship service. The pastor's auditorium class is virtually total teaching time. So, about 40 minutes is a good length for the class.

The pastor must teach the class.—Some people simply will come if the pastor teaches. Persons who cannot read or write will believe the pastor when he says that he will not call on them to read or speak, and the well educated will accept the pastor as being on their level. People who know a great deal in their area of expertise, but do not know the Bible, often are more comfortable in a pastor's auditorium class. Shy or introverted persons will like the pastor's auditorium class. The quality of teaching and the anonymity will appeal to baby boomers as well as many older persons.

Don't break your word.—If you say the class will be lecture, don't initiate discussion or ask questions that individuals would have to answer out loud. Don't call on people to pray or read. If you call on even one person, others will think, *He may call on me next time.*

Teach from the pulpit.—Teaching from the pulpit says that this is not just another class and that you expect the class to grow large. However, we are experiencing a growing trend today toward greater informality in the pulpit. In light of that, some pastors may want to move to a smaller lectern on the floor level with the people. Some feel that they can get closer to the people and use a more conversational style of teaching if they are on floor level. Some pastors even may want to do without a lectern. They feel that the lectern represents a barrier between themselves and the people.

The pastor's auditorium class is not a replacement for any other class. We need our graded Sunday School with men's, women's, and couples classes. This special class simply is a way of involving many people who are not now being reached by the church. Some members will stay in the pastor's auditorium class; but for many others, the class simply will be a nonthreatening entry point into the life of the church. Many members of this class will become future church leaders.

Focus on Special Events

Every Sunday morning ought to be a celebration of the resurrection of Jesus Christ. Church ought never to become routine or "business as usual." God's work is the most exciting work on the face of the earth. It is the only work that gets men, women, boys, and girls ready for heaven. Sunday morning, Sunday evening, Wednesday evening, and whatever other times the church meets are special times, but some occasions have unusual outreach potential. Do not let these rare opportunities slip by.

Plan big for revivals.—Early in my ministry, the settled belief was that churches that have two revivals a year baptize more than churches that have none or only one. Immediately, I determined that the churches I served would have two. I've never changed my mind about that. Even now revivals will work if we pray, plan, and participate properly. Pray for God's leadership in selecting your evangelist. Don't just invite a buddy. Invite the very best evangelist available, the one God most likely will use in your church. If the evangelist is your friend, fine; but above all, he should be gifted for what is needed in your church.

For weeks before the revival meeting, focus the congregation's attention on prayer. Pray for the revival in every service and in every Sunday School class or other group. Use a 24-hour prayer chain and prayer meetings in homes. Bathe the revival in prayer. At least six weeks before revival, preach continually toward the revival. If you are involved in a sermon series, keep preaching it; but let the revival so grip you that the revival will flow out in your illustrations and applications. Get the people to the revival by using a high attendance Sunday to begin the meeting. Use some method to promote attendance at the revival. Assign certain nights to Sunday School classes. Have "Youth Night," "Children's Night," and so forth. Use the pack-a-pew plan. Do not assume that people will come unless you promote the revival. Utilize the Saturday before the revival begins on Sunday to do a one-day soul winning seminar, including a blitz of the community. God will use revival meetings when we pray and prepare.

Promote special calendar events.—Easter is an obvious time to invite people to Sunday School and worship. The most successful experience in which I have been involved has been the enlistment of volunteers who the week before Easter call every home in the city or county (or your part of it) with an enthusiastic announcement of Sunday's services and an invitation to attend. In this approach, divide up the phone book so that persons are not called twice, but everyone is called once. These calls are not designed to get into discussions or to solicit names. They are designed simply to make the announcement in a pleasant, positive way and to thank them for listening. People are expecting to attend church at Easter more than at any other time of the year. Take advantage of the opportunity. Many new people can be reached.

Attendance on Mother's Day can be promoted by doing a baby (or parent) dedication service. Publicize the service in such a way that an invitation is communicated to parents and children who ordinarily do not attend church as well as those who do. Give a small gift to every baby (a New Testament, for example). You may want to promote the day by giving a gift to every mother present. You may want to have a special speaker or a parenting film. Always be careful with presentations not to offend women who would dearly love to be mothers but who have not been so blessed. Be sure to communicate good theology in the baby (or parent) dedication. Do not confuse this dedication with christening or baptism, and do not give false hope to parents who have little or no church background that the event has any saving grace. Follow up on prospects who are discovered through special Mother's Day events. Most of what has been said for Mother's Day can be applied to Father's Day, too.

These are just a few examples of what you can do to promote church attendance on special days. Other occasions such as Memorial Day can be a time for a ceremony or a sermon that will attract the unchurched. Musical celebrations around Independence Day and Christmas can draw new attenders. Look for innovative ways all year long to let the community know that they are wanted in your church.

Focus on various age groups and family needs. Have a Children's Day. Have a marriage vow renewal service for married couples. Conduct seminars on grief, divorce recovery, or living as a successful single. Invite a Christian sport star for a testimony appealing to youth. Have a special service honoring senior adults. The kinds of events that will attract new people are unlimited. Do not have so many of these that they get to be a parade, but many of these, correctly conducted, will attract unreached persons.

Maintain an Ongoing Outreach Visitation Program

An outreach visitation program can be as simple as a file box with 3 x 5 cards arranged alphabetically or as sophisticated as a computer program with coded information that will print out cards based on ages, sections of town, date last visited, and scores of other criteria. I have led and participated in both kinds of programs. The basics are not much different. The whole matter boils down to gathering names and addresses, maintaining up-to-date information, and, above all, having people who actually will make visits.

Some innovative ways and some good new ideas on outreach are available. But let me share a few basics with you.

The key to a successful outreach visitation program is to have a definite time to go, a time that you will not let other activities consume. In the churches where I have served, I made a genuine effort to schedule committee meetings and such on Sundays and Wednesdays and to ask the people for only one other night—visitation night—which we had either on Tuesday or Thursday. (Often our youth visited on Saturday.) I found it important to maintain this night for outreach visitation for my own benefit. Even the pastor gets so busy that if he does not discipline himself to a time to visit, the week will slip by without his doing any evangelistic visitation. If your church people and leaders know you are involved in visitation on Thursday night, they will respect your time and will not expect you to be somewhere else.

Gather around you those who will participate in visitation. Meet with them consistently. Make it a celebrative occasion. Make visits every week. Even if the number visiting is not large, it's amazing how many visits can be made. Also, the visitation effort can be increased if Sunday School classes can be encouraged to do ministry and absentee visitation, allowing the outreach night visits to focus on the lost, the unchurched, and prospects.

The kingdom leader inevitably is an administrator.

What if your church does not have a visitation program? Beginning a visitation program may be easier than refocusing one that has gotten off track. One of my last three churches had an outreach night that had drifted to the point where few outreach visits were being made. The other two churches had no visitation program.

How do you begin? Announce a time, make a commitment to be there yourself, and keep your commitment, week after week. Invite others to join you.

In one of my churches, I and my wife began the visitation program. By the time I left the church, on a typical Thursday night we had 16—all of them persons who had been reached through the visitation program. The group was not large, but it was very effective. The visitors had experienced the value of visitation. In another church, I began with about 12 visitors, and the number decreased to about four. Even that number was made up of people who were reached through visitation. Others soon captured the vision. The group was never large—about 20 most weeks and 50 on special occasions—but in five different years more than 100 were baptized in a town of about 8,000. So, don't be discouraged. Start with what you have. Be faithful yourself, and build a visitation team.

Be Open to New Methods

Recently, I have been involved in developing a new witnessing plan, the FAITH plan mentioned earlier in this chapter. I'm excited about this new resource. It systematizes what I have tried to practice for years. FAITH has grown out of the experience of First Baptist Church, Daytona Beach, Florida, under the leadership of its pastor, Dr. Bobby Welch, and it is being modeled in a number of our growing, evangelistic churches.

If I were a pastor today, I would become very familiar with this resource. Prayerfully consider whether it is a method God would bless in your church.

An openness to new methods will allow God to put before you an amazing array of plans, processes, and systems that He can and will bless in reaching the lost and discipling the saved.

Plan for the Future

Periodically review with your leadership the church's vision statement. Develop or review the church's strategic priorities, and develop action plans toward meeting the priorities. *Kingdom Principles Growth Strategies* by Gene Mims and Mike Miller is an extremely helpful tool for developing strategic priorities and evaluating progress toward them.

Look into next year, then into the next three to five years, and finally beyond five years. Ask, What is going to happen in my community. What does God have in mind for my church? What plans need to be put in place to accomplish what God has in mind? Begin to develop your calendar, to look at budgets, and to train your people. What God has in mind in your church will be so unique that I cannot suggest what will develop from your planning. I simply want to remind you not to miss out on what God has for you by failing to plan.

Use the Administrative Process.

A book by Alvin J. Lindgren titled *Foundations for Purposeful Church Administration* helps us understand that the kingdom leader inevitably is an administrator.[4] Some pastors, because of their views of spiritual leadership and a misunderstanding of administration, immediately recoil from this notion. Here the dictionary can help us. The word *administer* comes from the Latin words *ad* meaning "to," and *ministro* meaning "to serve." Therefore, an administrator is one who administers or ministers to others. Further, the word *administrator* means "one who manages, carries on or directs the affairs of any establishment or institution; a steward, manager, or acting governor." The kingdom leader is under appointment by God and is affirmed by the congregation in his calling as the administrator and leader of the greatest of institutions and organizations, the church, the body of Christ.

The wise kingdom leader will keep the church's mission before it at all times.

The following steps will help us to give kingdom style leadership.

Recognize the need.—For the need to be worthy of consideration, it must be related to the purpose of the church. If it is to claim the church's major attention and resources, it must be in line with the church's strategic priorities. The need may be to deal with poor stewardship, indifference to evangelism, or spiritual shallowness. Often needs are brought into focus by reviewing the end results that will occur as a result of a church being purpose driven and performing its functions in a balanced, healthy fashion. Those results are numerical growth, spiritual growth, expansion of ministries, and missions advance.

Plan to meet the need.—What are the possible solutions to the needs? Listen to the people. Perhaps gather a committee or task force. The problem should be clearly and concisely stated. Then gather the facts. Consider possible solutions. Evaluate the solutions until the very best one is agreed on. Present the plan to the church as a proposed solution to be adopted, further refined, or rejected.

Organize to carry out the adopted plan.—At this point, some of the following questions need to be asked and answered: What needs to be done to actualize the plan? When will we begin and finish? How will we gauge progress along the way? Who is going to carry out the various responsibilities? Who is going to guide the process, keep records, and be sure that follow-through occurs?

Stimulate and implement the process.—Implementation involves enlisting workers and training them. Next comes actually starting the process. Along the way encouragement will be needed. Communication with those directly involved—the task force or committee—and the congregation is vital. Proper supervision must occur.

Evaluate continually.—The plan continues to unfold as the process begins. When the project is concluded, evaluation is extremely important. Along the way adjustment inevitably will need to be made. More information may be gained. Personnel may fall by the wayside, or new gifts may be discovered. Progress needs to be monitored. When the project is completed, we must ask, Was the need met? Could the project have been done better? What did we learn about the people involved? Would we do things the same way or differently if we faced the same situation again? These questions and answers will be extremely valuable in the future.

Summary

The wise kingdom leader will keep the church's mission before it at all times. He will focus on the basics of church growth, and lead with his head and heart. He especially will stay tuned to the Holy Spirit's leadership.

---

[1] Gene Mims, *Kingdom Principles of Church Growth* (Nashville: Convention Press, 1994), 33.
[2] Article by John Clay, *Lexington (Kentucky) Herald-Leader,* 2 December 1996, sec. B, p. 1.
[3] J. N. Barnette, *A Church Using Its Sunday School* (Nashville: The Sunday School Board of the Southern Baptist Convention, 1951), 18.
[3] Alvin J. Lindgren, *Foundations for Purposeful Church Administration* (New York: Abingdon Press, 1965), 22, 70–84.